THE UNITED STATES AND CANADA:
THE QUEST FOR FREE TRADE

POLICY ANALYSES IN INTERNATIONAL ECONOMICS   16

THE UNITED STATES AND CANADA: THE QUEST FOR FREE TRADE

An Examination of
Selected Issues

Paul Wonnacott

With an Appendix by
John Williamson

92-1299

INSTITUTE FOR INTERNATIONAL ECONOMICS
WASHINGTON, DC
MARCH 1987

Paul Wonnacott, Professor of Economics at the University of Maryland, was a Visiting Fellow at the Institute in 1986. He has served on the staff of the Council of Economic Advisers (1968–70), the Federal Reserve Board (1974–75), and the US Treasury (1980). His publications include Free Trade Between the United States and Canada: The Potential Economic Effects *(with Ronald J. Wonnacott, 1967).*

INSTITUTE FOR INTERNATIONAL ECONOMICS
11 Dupont Circle, NW
Washington, DC 20036
(202) 328–9000 Telex: 248329 CEIP

C. Fred Bergsten, *Director*
Kathleen A. Lynch, *Director of Publications*
Ann L. Beasley, *Production Manager*

The Institute for International Economics was created, and is principally funded, by the German Marshall Fund of the United States.

The views expressed in this publication are those of the author. This publication is part of the overall program of the Institute, as endorsed by its Board of Directors, but does not necessarily reflect the views of individual members of the Board or the Advisory Committee.

Printed in the United States of America
91 90 89 88 87   5 4 3 2

Library of Congress Cataloging-in-Publication Data
Wonnacott, Paul.
  The United States and Canada.

  (Policy analyses in international economics; 16)
  References: p. 147
  1. United States—Foreign economic relations—Canada. 2. Canada—Foreign economic relations—United States. 3. United States—Commercial policy. 4. Canada—Commercial policy. 5. Free trade and protection. I. Title. II. Series.
HF1456.5.C2W65 1987   382.71073   87–2660
ISBN 0–88132–056–0

Contents

v

viii

Preface

Trade policy is a major focus of the research program of the Institute for International Economics. We have recently published four studies on wide-ranging components of the trade issue: the forthcoming round of multilateral trade negotiations, subsequently launched by the GATT membership at Punta del Este in September 1986; the domestic politics of trade policy in the United States and their impact on the outlook for trade legislation; domestic adjustment by American firms and workers to competition from abroad; and the crucial United States–Japan dimension of the overall problem.

In 1987, the Institute will be releasing several studies on more specific trade issues. Subsequent releases will cover two important sectors, agriculture and textiles/apparel (with later studies planned on steel and automobiles); a controversial new proposal, auctioning of import quotas; and "the politics of antiprotection," a heretofore neglected issue.

The analysis in this volume of *The United States and Canada: The Quest for Free Trade* is an appropriate initial release in this series. The United States and Canada conduct the largest two-way trade of any pair of countries in the world. Their negotiation is already underway, and both countries hope for a conclusion by late 1987. Recent disputes between them on specific products, including lumber and corn, have highlighted the case for new arrangements. And the outcome of these bilateral talks could have important precedential effects for the multilateral "Uruguay Round," in terms of both its overall prospects for success and on key individual issues such as rules governing services and the imposition of new trade barriers. In keeping with the traditional research approach of the Institute, the study attempts to integrate macroeconomic and exchange rate considerations with the more traditional components of trade policy.

The Institute for International Economics is a private nonprofit research institution for the study and discussion of international

xi

economic policy. Its purpose is to analyze important issues in that area, and to develop and communicate practical new approaches for dealing with them. The Institute is completely nonpartisan.

The Institute was created by a generous commitment of funds from the German Marshall Fund of the United States in 1981, and continues to receive substantial support from that source. In addition, major institutional grants are now being received from the Ford Foundation, the William and Flora Hewlett Foundation, and the Alfred P. Sloan Foundation. The Dayton Hudson Foundation provides partial support for the Institute's program of studies on trade policy. A number of other foundations and private corporations are contributing to the increasing diversification of the Institute's financial resources.

The Board of Directors bears overall responsibility for the Institute and gives general guidance and approval to its research program—including identification of topics that are likely to become important to international economic policymakers over the medium run (generally, one to three years) and which thus should be addressed by the Institute. The Director, working closely with the staff and outside Advisory Committee, is responsible for the development of particular projects and makes the final decision to publish an individual study.

The Institute hopes that its studies and other activities will contribute to building a stronger foundation for international economic policy around the world. Comments as to how it can best do so are invited from readers of these publications.

C. FRED BERGSTEN
Director
February 1987

1 US-Canadian Free Trade: The Issue That Will Not Die

On March 17, 1985, President Ronald W. Reagan and Prime Minister Brian Mulroney met in Quebec City, in what was known as the "Shamrock Summit," both because of the Irish ancestry of the two main participants and because they met on St. Patrick's Day.

As part of their communique, the President and the Prime Minister announced their agreement "to give the highest priority to finding mutually acceptable means to reduce and eliminate existing barriers to trade in order to secure and facilitate trade and investment flows." William E. Brock, the US Trade Representative, and James F. Kelleher, the Canadian Minister for International Trade, were directed to "chart all possible ways to reduce and eliminate existing barriers to trade," and to report within six months.

Six months later, on September 26, the Prime Minister informed the House of Commons that he had spoken to the President "to express Canada's interests in pursuing a new trade agreement between our two countries." Canada would "seek to negotiate the broadest possible package of mutually beneficial reductions in tariffs and nontariff barriers between our two countries."

With this Canadian initiative, the ball was in the US court. Under the Trade and Tariff Act of 1984, the President was required to notify the House Ways and Means Committee and the Senate Finance Committee of any request by a foreign government for free trade negotiations with the United States. If, after consultations with the executive branch, neither committee disapproved within 60 days, negotiations could begin under the "fast-track" procedure, under which any resulting agreement would receive expedited consideration: the House and Senate would be committed to vote the agreement and implementing legislation up or down without amendment. The first hurdle—the 60-day period of possible disapproval—was overcome,

1

but just barely: the Finance Committee agreed to let the negotiations proceed, but only by a vote of 10 to 10. With this rather inauspicious background, a series of trade negotiations began in May 1986, to investigate the prospects for a reduction in trade barriers, possibly ending in a comprehensive free trade arrangement.

It should come as no surprise that the world's two closest trading partners should have much to discuss. Their bilateral merchandise trade in 1985 totaled US$125 billion (exports plus imports), compared to $88 billion between the United States and Japan, and $108 billion between the United States and the 10 members of the European Community (EC).[1] In the two years 1984–85, Canada bought 22 percent of US exports, or more than twice as much as second-placed Japan. Indeed, if Canada were considered as two separate countries—the first being Ontario, and the second the other nine provinces—Ontario would be the leading buyer of US exports, with the remaining nine provinces ranking in third place, ahead of Mexico and Britain.

And, if Canada is the largest trading partner of the United States, the United States has a much greater—indeed, a preponderant—influence on the Canadian economy. Merchandise exports constitute a full 25 percent of Canadian GNP, with almost 80 percent of these exports going to the United States. To survive, many Canadian business executives must keep one eye focused across the border, and the Canadian government must likewise pay attention to US developments in deciding on a whole range of policies, from macroeconomic management to trade policy. For example, when the US Congress recently passed a comprehensive tax bill, the possibility of tax reform became a more active issue in Canada. The Canadian view—that they live in the overwhelming presence of their giant neighbor to the south—was summed up by former Prime Minister Pierre Trudeau. Living next to the United States, he said, was somewhat similar to sleeping next to an elephant. No matter how good-natured the beast, one does tend to notice every grunt and twitch.[2]

---

1. "Dollars" are US dollars, unless otherwise noted.
2. Porfirio Diaz, the Mexican president prior to World War I, was less tactful: "Poor Mexico! So far from God, and so close to the United States."

Issues for Negotiation

In negotiations for free trade, a number of topics arise: tariffs, nontariff barriers, and trade remedy laws as well as the related issues of services, investment, and exchange rates.

TARIFFS

Tariffs are the traditional, and most obvious, barrier to trade; free trade would require an elimination of tariffs on trade between the United States and Canada.

Already, most of the trade between the two countries is duty free—about 65 percent of US exports, and 80 percent of US imports. By the end of the Tokyo round tariff cuts in 1987, an additional 25 percent of US exports and 15 percent of US imports from Canada will face tariffs of 5 percent or less. As a result, it is sometimes argued that tariffs have become unimportant as barriers to trade between the two nations. However, these percentages give a misleading impression regarding the freedom of trade. Specifically, they do not take into account the trade that might have occurred, but which has been suppressed by tariff barriers. In an extreme example, if two countries had zero tariffs on half of each other's products, and prohibitive tariffs on the other half, then 100 percent of actual trade between them would be duty free. The average tariff, weighted according to actual imports, would be zero. But tariffs would nevertheless constitute important barriers to trade; in this example, they would suppress half of the potential trade.

Although the average level of tariffs between Canada and the United States is not high, there are high tariffs in some industries. Observe, in table 1.1, the double-digit Canadian tariffs on textiles, wearing apparel, footwear, and furniture. In each of these industries except furniture, US tariffs also exceed 7 percent. Furthermore, the industry averages are biased downward for the reason explained in the previous paragraph: they are weighted according to actual imports. Where extra-high tariffs block the import of specific items, those items are given little weight in calculating the industry average. For example, US

TABLE 1.1   **Tariffs by industrial sector, post-Tokyo Round, 1987 (percentage)**

	Canada	United States
Textiles	16.9	7.2
Clothing	23.7	18.4
Leather products	4.0	2.5
Footwear	21.5	9.0
Wood products	2.5	0.2
Furniture and fixtures	14.3	4.6
Paper products	6.6	0.0
Printing and publishing	1.1	0.3
Chemicals	7.9	0.6
Petroleum products	0.4	0.0
Rubber products	7.3	3.2
Nonmetal mineral products	4.4	0.3
Glass products	6.9	5.7
Iron and steel	5.1	2.7
Nonferrous metals	3.3	0.5
Metal products	8.6	4.0
Nonelectrical machinery	4.6	2.2
Electrical machinery	7.5	4.5
Transportation equipment	0.0	0.0
Miscellaneous manufactures	5.0	0.9

Note: Canadian tariff averages are weighted by imports from the United States, and vice versa.

Source: Brown and Stern (1987, table 2), based on information supplied by Office of US Trade Representative.

tariffs of 20 percent on plywood and 18 percent on methanol (a primary petrochemical) are given little weight in calculating industry averages.

It will be argued in later chapters that much of the specialization that would occur in the event of bilateral free trade would take place *within* industries. The principal reason is that, in many industries, economies of large-scale production cannot be fully achieved within the limited Canadian domestic market. For example, in the furniture industry—where style and choice are important—the Canadian industry is driven to produce a wide variety of products, each in small numbers, in order to meet consumer demand. In the event of bilateral free trade, there would be pressures on the Canadian industry to specialize in relatively few products, producing them for both the Canadian and US markets, and to retire from other products, leaving the Canadian domestic market in these items to imports.

Of course, some intraindustry specialization can occur even in the presence of tariffs. But, for such two-way specialization to occur, the cost differentials between items that Canada exports and those that Canada imports would have to be enough to cover *both* US and Canadian tariffs—in the furniture case, about 19 percent. The reason is that Canadian costs in the items of Canadian specialization would have to be at least 4.6 percent *less* than US costs, if Canadian exporters were to compete in the US market after the payment of duties. At the same time, Canadian producers would have an incentive to retire from other domestic market segments only if their costs in those items were more than 14.3 percent *higher* than US costs; otherwise, they would be protected by the Canadian tariff. In brief, intraindustry specialization—and other specialization, for that matter—is inhibited by *both* sets of tariffs.

The significance of tariffs as a barrier to trade has been illustrated by what has happened in the automobile industry over the past quarter century. In 1965, a bilateral agreement between the United States and Canada provided for duty-free trade in new automobiles and original-equipment parts. Since that time, bilateral trade in these items has increased sharply, from an annual average of $625 million in 1963–64 (only 0.1 percent of US GNP) to an annual average of $42 billion in 1984–85 (1.1 percent of US GNP). Between 1980 and 1985, automotive trade accounted for $25 billion of the overall increase of $40 billion in two-way trade.

Tariffs are reasonably uncomplicated. Although each country would like its trading partners to lower their tariffs, tariffs are relatively unlikely to create misunderstandings, controversy, and passion. They are unlikely to dominate discussions over trade policy. Indeed, most of this study will deal with more complex issues such as nontariff barriers and the treatment of subsidies, where perceptions may be quite different on the two sides of the border, and major misunderstandings can occur. Therefore, a preliminary point is worth particular emphasis. *Tariffs do matter.* Even low tariffs—of, say, 5 percent on trade in each direction—can inhibit specialization. The elimination of tariffs can be an important part of a bilateral agreement between the United States and Canada.

NONTARIFF BARRIERS

As tariffs have been gradually lowered in recent decades, other barriers to trade have gained in relative importance. Nontariff barriers (NTBs) include quotas, "voluntary" export restraints (in products such as textiles, steel, and automobiles), government marketing boards (particularly in agricultural products), and the outright prohibition of imports, often as a part of an agricultural price-support system (though sometimes also applied to other products, such as the Canadian prohibition on imports of used cars). Perhaps the most important NTB is created by government procurement policies; national or local suppliers are generally given preference.

NTBs are numerous, and at times subtle. Indeed, some exist within countries—such as preferences for local contractors by cities, or provincial marketing boards. Even within Canada and the United States, completely free trade does not exist, in spite of the constitutional prohibition on internal tariffs. This is one reason why some prefer to talk of "freer trade," and avoid the term "free trade" altogether. We will use the term "free trade" to mean substantially free trade—the elimination of tariffs and the reduction of NTBs, even though perfectly free trade is not a realistic prospect.

TRADE REMEDY LAWS

As tariff rates have been negotiated downward in recent decades, countries have become increasingly concerned that their domestic industries might be subject to excessive or unfair foreign competition. In response, they have extended and tightened their trade remedy laws.

US trade remedy laws take four major forms:

• escape clause actions, where imports are causing (or threatening) serious injury to a domestic industry

• antidumping duties

• countervailing duties to compensate for foreign subsidies

• restrictions on imports where foreign countries are engaged in unfair practices (for example, patent infringements).

All four forms are generally grouped together under the heading, "trade remedy laws," but there is a fundamental difference between the first and the last three. The first is aimed at providing temporary *protection* against severe foreign competition; there is no need for the complaining domestic industry to prove any misbehavior on the part of foreign exporters. In contrast, the last three are intended to provide relief from *unfair* foreign practices, such as dumping or subsidies. The first is designed to provide a *temporary cushion* in the process of adjusting to the changing international pattern of comparative advantage. The purpose of the last three is to compensate for foreign subsidies and other distortions, and thus allow trade patterns to correspond *more closely* to the underlying forces of comparative advantage.

However, there is a widespread view in Canada that US trade remedy laws are being used as a backdoor form of protection. This is especially true of the countervailing duty (CVD) law, where Canadians perceive a US tendency to define subsidies more and more broadly as an excuse for imposing protective tariffs. When low-priced raw materials are deemed subsidies—as in the recent softwood lumber case—Canadians believe that it is particularly likely that the application of CVD will interfere with efficient international specialization.

Furthermore, US trade remedy laws are seen as a very difficult problem in Canada because they make access to the US market *less predictable*. Yet *predictable* and *assured* access to the US market is critically important if Canadian industry is to specialize in large-scale production aimed at capturing segments of the North American market. Accordingly, a major objective of Canada in the current negotiations is to limit the application of US trade remedy laws. On the other side, the United States wants to negotiate limits on Canadian subsidies that can lead to countervailing actions. This is not to suggest that subsidies and countervailing actions are all one-sided. The United States also has subsidies that can lead to countervailing duty petitions—as in the current Canadian case against US corn exports. The point is that the primary Canadian concern is with US countervailing duties, rather than subsidized exports to Canada, while the primary US concern is with Canadian subsidies, not with Canadian CVD actions.

SERVICES

Freer trade can lead to more competitive markets, and to the more efficient production of goods. The same is true for services, such as tourism, financial services (for example, banking and insurance), professional consulting (for example, engineering, construction), computer services, and advertising.

Both sides have expressed interest in services. The United States has for some time wanted an extension of trade discussions to include services. An agreement on services is an important US objective in the current negotiations within the General Agreement on Tariffs and Trade (GATT), and the recent free trade agreement between the United States and Israel included a broad statement of principles whose purpose is to provide a basis for specific agreements on services. The United States would welcome bilateral progress on services with Canada, both in its own right and as a precedent for negotiations with other countries. In Canada, a major bank (the Royal Bank) has suggested liberalized international access to computer services (Frazee 1983 and Grey 1983b). Nevertheless, there are significant reservations regarding services, particularly where the maintenance of a Canadian national culture is at stake. For example, Canada has discouraged its firms from using US television stations along the border for advertisements aimed at the domestic Canadian market, in order to support Canadian advertising media, and Canadian broadcasters have been required to include Canadian content in their programs. The view is very strong in Canada that a degree of economic inefficiency is not too high a price to pay for cultural independence, and this is likely to prevent a comprehensive agreement on services.

Royalties on patents and other intellectual property are also sometimes classified as a service. The United States has complained to

Canada about the compulsory licensing of pharmaceuticals at an artificially low royalty of 4 percent. Negotiations on this item have recently led the Canadian government to agree to changes in the law.

INVESTMENT

Trade and investment are related. For example, the decision of foreign nations to invest in a country can create a demand for imported machinery, and it can provide the foreign exchange to finance such imports. After the investment has taken place, the resulting production can add to the supply of exports and of import-competing products. Agreements to eliminate tariffs are sometimes accompanied by commitments to lower barriers on international investment, as in the case of the European Common Market.

To form a free trade association, as contrasted to a common market, it is not necessary to free international capital movements. Nevertheless, it is appropriate, when trade barriers are under negotiation, to also consider barriers to international investment. One particular barrier is likely to be a subject of negotiations in the current US-Canadian talks—namely the performance requirements that have in the past been imposed on foreign firms investing in Canada. Where investing firms must meet domestic content requirements, a nontariff barrier to imports is created. Where firms are required to meet export targets, the results may be similar to subsidies on exports.

EXCHANGE RATES

The efficiency gains from free trade require an environment in which the competitive positions of different producers reflect their comparative advantage. This tends to be the case within a country, where there is a single currency—although even within a single country, pockets of market power and other imperfections can distort relative prices. Across national boundaries, exchange rate changes introduce an additional complication.

An exchange rate change can act as part of the adjustment process. For example, the currency of a country with a weak current account balance will generally tend to depreciate, restoring its competitive position. If countries are to have a degree of autonomy in macroeconomic policies, exchange rate adjustments may be essential as a way of preventing progressively larger imbalances in international payments. But changes in exchange rates may not only reduce pressures on the payments system; they can also create problems. Volatile movements of international capital can produce sharp movements in exchange rates that produce shifts in competitive positions that do not reflect underlying changes in the real economy. In recent years, exchange rates have become seriously misaligned for extended periods. Such misalignments have contributed to the large current account deficits of the United States.

Because exchange rates can have a powerful effect on trading relationships, the question arises as to whether, and how, exchange rate issues might be dealt with in a bilateral US-Canadian negotiation. Traditionally, exchange rates have been dealt with separately from trade matters—the former through the International Monetary Fund (IMF) and meetings of small groups of countries, and the latter through the GATT and bilateral negotiations. Because trade negotiations and exchange rate matters can each be rather complex, this traditional division of topics makes sense. In the present case, the US-Canadian trade negotiations are sufficiently difficult by themselves not to be complicated further by exchange rate issues. The Group of Five has on occasion been expanded to Seven—to include Canada and Italy—and this would seem to be an appropriate forum within which the US-Canadian exchange rate can be discussed. Nevertheless, the exchange rate between the US and Canadian dollars will be briefly considered in this study (chapter 5) for a number of reasons: it can affect the workings of a free trade agreement; it can affect the political acceptability of an agreement; and its possible misalignment has recently been raised by the Congress and by US Trade Representative Clayton K. Yeutter.

OUTLINE OF THIS STUDY

The second chapter of this study will deal with the potential gains from a bilateral free trade agreement. The third chapter will address the question of why bilateral free trade—which has been a recurring issue in US-Canadian relations for over a hundred years—has once again become a matter of negotiation. The fourth chapter will address one of the principal areas where agreement may be difficult, namely, the application of trade remedy laws. Chapter 5 will consider the coverage of an agreement, including topics such as services and investment. Chapter 6 will present a summary of the principal conclusions. Throughout—and particularly in chapter 4—I have attempted to explore selected problems in sufficient detail for the reader to understand why they are problems, and why solutions may be difficult. Because of this in-depth study of selected problems, the number of pages should not be taken as a measure of the importance of various topics. To warn the reader of this somewhat uneven treatment, the study has been subtitled, "An Examination of Selected Issues."

But first, a brief historical summary of the free trade issue will be provided.

The Issue That Will Not Die

Trade with the United States has played a central and continuing role in Canadian politics. Indeed, changing trade relationships with the United States were a major reason for the unification of the provinces into the Canadian nation in 1867. "Reciprocity"—bilateral free trade with the United States—was the issue on which the Liberal Party went down to defeat in the election of 1911. But even the Liberals' electoral disaster could not kill the reciprocity issue; it has periodically been revived.[3]

---

3. In the history of US-Canadian relations, the term "reciprocity" has had a meaning different from that in the recent US internal debate on commercial policy. Historically, "reciprocity" has meant an agreement for bilateral US-Canadian free trade, covering at least a sizable share of trade. In the recent US debate over commercial policy, reciprocity means an insistence on access to foreign markets equal to foreign access to the US market. The implication is that foreign access to US markets would be restricted where foreign countries are unwilling to grant reciprocal access. In this study, "reciprocity" is used in the traditional sense in which it has appeared in the history of US-Canadian commercial policy. For a discussion of the other type of "reciprocity," see Cline (1982).

Briefly, these are the historical highlights.[4] When the Peel Government in Britain repealed the Corn Laws in the mid-nineteenth century, moving toward unilateral free trade, business in Canada was adversely affected. No longer did Canadian exports enjoy substantial preferences as they entered the British market. Feeling foresaken by the Empire, Canadians responded in two ways. One was a "tit-for-tat." British preferences in the Canadian market were almost eliminated by a combined increase of duties on British goods and a reduction of duties on American products in 1847. The second response was sharper—a move to become even more closely tied with the United States than with Britain. Many of the business elite of Montreal joined the Annexation movement of 1849, aimed at an outright union with the United States. Less drastically, overtures were made for bilateral free trade with the United States. In 1851, early negotiations failed in the face of US indifference. But by 1854, there was something the United States very much wanted—fishing rights off the east coast. A deal was done; a Reciprocity Treaty was entered, providing for free trade in natural products between the two countries. Quickly, the United States replaced Britain as Canada's principal trading partner.

However, the relationship between the United States and Canada soured during the Civil War. The United States resented British support for the Confederate States, and took out its resentments on Canada; the Reciprocity Treaty was abrogated in 1866. Forsaken by Britain, and rebuffed by the United States, the Canadian provinces looked to one another. In 1867, they joined hands in Confederation, forming the Canadian nation stretching "*a mari usque ad mare*" (the Canadian motto, meaning "from sea to sea").

But confederation did not settle the question of commercial policy. The US market still lured, and the Canadian government sent a representative to Washington to negotiate a new reciprocity treaty in 1874. It died in the Senate. The pendulum then swung in the other direction, with the Conservative victory in 1878 and the introduction of Prime Minister John A. Macdonald's "National Policy." But even this strongly protectionist move reflected an ambivalence; perhaps Canadian tariffs could be used as a bargaining lever to persuade

---

4. For more details, see Granatstein (1985); Reisman (1984); and Young (1957).

Americans to lower their tariffs. In explaining his tariff policy, Macdonald argued that:

It is only by closing our doors and by cutting them out of our markets that they will open theirs to us.[5]

This theme was to be repeated a half century later, during the election campaign of 1930. Conservative leader R.B. Bennett—who was about to win the election and become Prime Minister—justified high Canadian tariffs to a Winnipeg audience:

You say our tariffs are only for the manufacturers. I will make them fight for you as well. I will use them to blast a way into the markets that have been closed to you.[6]

This was one of the central, recurring problems of Canadian commercial policy: how to get US attention in negotiations for lower tariffs. Another was whether Canada really wanted lower tariffs—a matter on which public opinion and the Canadian government blew hot and cold. By the late 1880s, the pendulum was swinging back toward a deal with the United States. Two phrases became common in public debate—"commercial union" (what would now be called a customs union; that is, free trade with a common external tariff) and "unrestricted reciprocity" (what would now be called a free trade area, with each country maintaining its tariffs on imports from the outside). But again Canadian overtures were rebuffed in Washington, with Secretary of State James Blaine being particularly blunt:

I am opposed, teetotally opposed, to giving the Canadians the sentimental satisfaction of waving the British flag, paying British taxes [sic], and enjoying the actual cash remuneration of American markets. They cannot have both at the same time.[7]

In Canada, the periodic debate over reciprocity has touched two sensitive nerves. One has been the regional diversity of Canada. The west, as an exporter of natural products, has had an interest in freer trade as a way of getting cheap manufactures. The central manufacturing area favored a more protectionist policy, to stimulate its industrial

---

5. *Debates,* House of Commons, 7 March 1878, as quoted by Granatstein (1985, p. 17).
6. As quoted by Colombo (1974).
7. Waite (1971), p. 223.

growth. When a new Reciprocity Treaty was negotiated in 1911, it provided for free trade in natural products, with a lowering of tariffs on manufactures. This was seen as the thin edge of the wedge by Ontario industrialists, who feared the eventual elimination of their tariff protection. A group of Toronto business executives provided the rallying cry for the antireciprocity forces in the election of 1911: "No Truck Nor Trade with the Yankees."

The second nerve was even more sensitive: were free traders selling out their country? Would free trade inevitably lead to political union with the United States? In 1911, Speaker-designate Champ Clark of the House of Representatives suggested that the answer might be yes: he expressed his hope to see the US flag floating over Canada. The Liberals lost the election, taking down the Reciprocity Treaty with them.

The sensitivity of these two points has persisted into the recent Canadian debate. In each case, proponents of free trade argue that fears are exaggerated. They argue that free trade is desirable not only for the regions that export raw materials; it is also desirable if Canada is to have a healthy, highly productive manufacturing sector.[8] In spite of the traditional Canadian fear of becoming mere "hewers of wood and drawers of water" for Americans, this will not happen with free trade. The main points in this case will be considered in chapter 2. Nevertheless, concerns persist over the competitiveness of Canadian industry in a free trade area. Of the provinces, Ontario is perhaps the least favorably disposed toward bilateral free trade, and an important test for Canadian negotiators will be whether they can gain Ontario's approval of an agreement.

Proponents of free trade also argue that it is consistent with the continuing political independence of Canada. The European Free Trade Association (EFTA) established the precedent of a free trade arrangement in which each country maintained its own tariff on imports

---

8. Indeed, Shearer, Young, and Munro (1971, p. 203), estimate that free trade among the North Atlantic nations would raise the incomes of the industrialized regions of Canada even more than it would raise the incomes in British Columbia. (For BC, they estimate a gain in the 4 percent to 7 percent range.) They conclude that:

Western Canada—and specifically British Columbia—suffers from being in a customs union with the rest of the country; the central provinces suffer from not being in a customs union with the rest of the world.

from third countries; a free trade agreement with the United States would not require Canadian tariff policy to be made in Washington. Even the European Community—a much tighter arrangement with common external tariffs—has been consistent with the survival of the member countries as separate policy-making units. Indeed, one of the problems of the EC is that the development of a true "common market" has in fact been exceedingly difficult. Particularly in telecommunications and other areas of high tech, governments have been reluctant to allow market forces to work; procurement and development policies have kept the European market fragmented. But, in spite of the evidence that free trade is consistent with the survival of nations as independent units, opponents of bilateral free trade have warned of US domination. Shirley Carr, President of the Canadian Labour Congress, provided a recent example:

It is in the interest of the United States to try to take over Canada. It has always been, ever since Canada was first formed. . . . They want to disrupt and disturb everything we have and bring us down to their level.[9]

FREE TRADE NEGOTIATIONS OF 1947–48

Following the Liberal debacle at the polls in 1911, the free trade issue was for many years too hot for political parties to touch. However, the era of good will at the end of the World War II set the stage for new initiatives. In 1944, the two countries agreed to eliminate tariffs on agricultural machinery, thereby reducing the grievances of the western provinces over Canadian tariff policy. In 1947, the two countries entered confidential negotiations aimed at free trade. By March 1948, a draft agreement had been reached, including:

- an immediate elimination of tariffs

- transitional quotas over a five-year period

- thereafter, quotas would be prohibited with two exceptions: US quotas on wheat and flour, and seasonal Canadian quotas on fresh fruits and vegetables

9. Interview, 17 August 1986, as reported by the Canadian Press.

• provision for joint consultation, particularly to work out joint marketing agreements for agricultural products.

Prime Minister Mackenzie King had given the green light for the negotiations, and his initial reaction to the draft agreement was favorable. But he felt uneasy about the magnitude of the decision. It would, he wrote in his diary, be about as significant as any step that a government might take, short of war. "Its possibilities are so far-reaching for good on one hand, but possible disaster if project were defeated that I find it necessary to reflect a good deal before attempting final decision." Caution prevailed; King decided not to go ahead.

THE RECENT REVIVAL OF INTEREST IN BILATERAL FREE TRADE

In spite of King's rejection of the draft agreement for free trade, the Canadian economy continued to be heavily dependent on the United States. In the mid 1950s, about three-fifths of Canadian exports went to the United States, and almost three-quarters of Canadian imports came from the States.

This heavy dependence on the United States tugged Canadian policy in two conflicting directions. One response was to attempt to escape, at least partially, from the US orbit. In the late 1950s, Conservative Prime Minister John Diefenbaker pledged to shift 15 percent of Canada's trade from the United States to Britain—a pledge that turned out to be utterly unrealistic. By the 1970s, Liberal Prime Minister Pierre Trudeau was pursuing the "Third Option," of switching some of Canada's trade away from the United States and toward Europe and the developing countries.[10] (The first option was the status quo; the second was a closer relationship with the United States.) Again, this policy proved easier to proclaim than to implement. Efforts to promote closer ties with Europe were a failure; the share of Canadian exports going to Western Europe declined from 19 percent in 1970 to 15 percent in 1980 and 7 percent in 1985.

The other response was to look once more at the "Second Option"— a closer relationship with the United States, and, in particular, steps to enhance Canadian access to the lucrative US market. In 1958, the

---

10. On the third option, see the paper by Mitchell Sharp (1972).

two countries negotiated the Defense Production Sharing Agreement, increasing the ability of Canadian firms to compete for US defense contracts, and acting as a balance-of-payments offset to heavy US purchases by the Canadian armed forces. In 1965, the two nations entered into the Auto Pact, providing duty-free trade in new cars and original equipment parts. However, this agreement was inspired not so much by any grand free trade design, but rather by an attempt to avoid an open conflict over Canadian subsidies to automotive exports. Nevertheless, it led to a rapid increase in two-way trade.

A combination of factors contributed to the reemergence of the free trade option. One was the increasing awareness of the business community, academics, and politicians of how difficult it is for Canadian manufacturing to achieve large-scale, efficient production without assured access to a large market.[11] With British entry into the European Community, Canada was seen as suffering a major disadvantage as one of a very few industrialized non-socialist countries without unfettered access to a market of at least 100 million consumers. One senior corporate executive described the problem of Canadian business:

We, manufacturers, are caught in a Catch-22 situation. On the one hand, the tariffs in Canada are no longer high enough to offset the higher costs of producing solely for the Canadian market. On the other hand, even modest tariffs into the US can make it difficult, if not impossible, to set up production in Canada to export into that market.[12]

Another contributing factor in the reemergence of the free trade option was the fear—which grew rapidly as US trade deficits mushroomed in the early 1980s—that the United States might be sliding back into protectionism, with potentially devastating consequences for Canadian exports. With the increasing diversification of Canadian exports away from raw materials, and toward manufactured products, Canada was becoming increasingly vulnerable to US protection. A bilateral deal might ensure Canadian access to the US market. Finally,

---

11. Academic works that emphasized the problem of achieving efficient production in a small market include Eastman and Stykolt (1967), English (1964), Harris and Cox (1984), and Wonnacott and Wonnacott (1967). The advantages to Canada of a bilateral free trade agreement are summarized in Lipsey and Smith (1985).

12. J.E. Newall, Chairman, DuPont Canada Inc., as quoted in Royal Commission. . . (1985, p. 300).

and most important, politicians in both parties showed increasing willingness to reconsider a reciprocal movement toward freer trade, in spite of its obvious political dangers. An early step was taken by the Canadian Senate, an appointed body whose lifetime tenure provides some insulation from political storms. In 1982, the Standing Senate Committee on Foreign Affairs, under the chairmanship of Senator George C. van Roggen, suggested that a free trade agreement be considered. In 1983, the Trudeau government published a review of trade policy, proposing the negotiation of bilateral sectoral agreements with the United States. In August 1985, the Royal Commission on the Economic Union and Development Prospects for Canada (the Macdonald Commission) broadened the free trade discussion:

Successive rounds of GATT negotiations have traditionally provided Canada and the United States with the main opportunities to liberalize cross-border trade. Future negotiations could well offer new opportunities to liberalize and secure Canada-U.S. bilateral trade. Such negotiations, however, are unlikely to take place soon enough or to be thorough enough or provide the kind of environment Canadian producers will need by the end of the decade and beyond. We need, therefore, to engage the United States more directly in bilateral free trade negotiations.[13]

Both major political parties had members who looked favorably on a prospective free trade agreement. The Chairman of the Royal Commission, Donald Macdonald, was Minister of Finance under the Liberal Government of Pierre Trudeau. The free trade initiative was taken in 1985 by Prime Minister Brian Mulroney, leader of the traditionally protectionist Conservative Party. At least in the early stages, the current free trade debate has taken place within parties, rather than between them. That does not, however, lessen the courage needed for a free trade initiative. Seventy-five years ago, one Canadian government was defeated at the polls on the Reciprocity issue. We may hope that history will not repeat itself. But we cannot be sure. The political danger will put pressures on negotiators on both sides of the border to succeed. However, it may also make compromise difficult, and may lead Canada to break off talks (or to severely limit their

---

13. Royal Commission . . . (1985, p. 374). On the recent changes in attitudes, see the paper by Sperry Lea, "What a Difference Twenty-One Years Make" (1987).

scope—to government procurement policies, for example) if a politically acceptable agreement seems unattainable.

In the United States, preliminary steps were simultaneously being taken to clear the way for bilateral agreements. One hope was that, by negotiating agreements with its neighbors, the United States could demonstrate that progress was possible, and set the stage for broader multilateral negotiations, particularly in new areas such as services and the protection of intellectual property. Section 1104 of the Trade Agreements Act of 1979 specifically charged the President with studying "the desirability of entering into trade agreements with countries in the northern portion of the western hemisphere to promote . . . the mutual expansion of market opportunities." The resulting report by the US Trade Representative (1981, p. 2) concluded that it seemed appropriate to improve trade relations with Mexico and Canada separately, rather than on a broad regional basis. The report noted (p. 3) the integration and rationalization that had occurred in the automobile industry since the 1965 pact and concluded that "further opportunities to rationalize industries through freer trade should be explored."

The two governments in fact agreed upon four sectors for negotiations—surface transportation procurement, informatics, agricultural equipment, and steel. However, negotiations never actually began. There were several problems with the sectoral approach: it could lead to jockeying between the two countries for the inclusion of industries where one of the countries had a particularly strong competitive position; it could lead to a proliferation of specific industry safeguards such as those that accompanied the automotive pact; it would have been inconsistent with the commitments of the two countries under GATT Article XXIV; and it would have meant a very slow and arduous reduction in trade barriers.[14] The stage was set for Prime Minister Mulroney's initiative of September 1985.

---

14. On the sectoral approach, see Hufbauer and Samet (1985).

2 Bilateral Free Trade: The Sources of Gain

Nobody seriously suggests that the United States would be more prosperous if there were an impenetrable wall around the nation, keeping out all imports and preventing all exports. It is obvious that we gain from exporting wheat and manufactured products, in order to be able to pay for imports of goods like coffee or bananas which could be produced not at all, or only at extremely high cost, in the United States. Similarly, there are obvious gains from importing nickel, chromium, and other raw materials either absent or in short supply in the United States.

But to show that we gain from *some* trade does not demonstrate that we would do best with completely unfettered, free trade. Commercial policy—the setting of tariffs and other impediments to international trade, and the negotiation with other countries over the terms of access to their markets—raises complex and subtle issues, particularly when bilateral rather than multilateral, most-favored-nation (MFN) tariff reductions are under consideration. Commercial policy is rightly a matter of continuing debate. In this debate, economic theory and quantitative estimates can provide important insights and information. But in most cases they are incapable of producing answers that are categorically "correct" and beyond dispute. In his classic *Studies in the Theory of International Trade* (1937, p. 593), Jacob Viner—an expatriate Canadian who taught at the University of Chicago and Princeton—summarized the international economic theory of the preceding century. His conclusions were modest, perhaps disappointingly so: "The theory of international trade, at its best, can provide only presumptions, not demonstrations, as to the benefit or injury to be expected. . . ."

This chapter has four major purposes:

- to summarize the empirical work of economists who have looked at

21

the effects of bilateral US-Canadian free trade on real incomes to see what "presumptions" and insights they provide

• to consider the effects of bilateral free trade on specific industries, particularly those that are likely to face the severest import competition

• to consider the issue of "fairness" in international trade negotiations

• to study the effects of a bilateral arrangement on broader trade policy, and, in particular, to look at the implications of departures from the most-favored-nation principle that lies at the heart of the General Agreement on Tariffs and Trade (GATT). (According to the MFN principle, any tariff concession granted to one trading partner is extended to all GATT members.)

Free Trade: Quantitative Effects

Empirical work has generally indicated that bilateral free trade would result in higher real incomes in the two countries, particularly Canada. However, the estimates of the size of the gain, and the distribution of the gain between the two countries, vary widely among the empirical studies, largely because they use different methodologies and are based on different assumptions.

Traditionally, the gains from reducing trade barriers have been estimated within a relatively simple framework, whose underlying assumptions include perfectly competitive markets and *constant returns to scale*; that is, there are no cost advantages in large-scale production. This simple framework is sufficient to pick up an important source of gains from trade, namely, those identified in the classical theory of comparative advantage. Fundamental differences—such as those in climate, raw material endowments, technology, and quantities of capital—cause differences in relative prices between nations, which in turn create the incentive for trade. Thus, for example, differences in climate and soil explain why Brazil is a low-cost producer of coffee, and the United States of wheat. Countries gain by exporting their products of comparative advantage, to pay for low-cost imports from foreign countries.

A substantially more complicated and difficult approach includes the economies of large-scale production. Such economies can provide a powerful incentive to trade, and a significant additional source of gain. One reason for *economies of scale* is the existence of large overheads and fixed costs; there is an advantage in exporting to foreign markets to spread fixed costs. Thus, for example, Boeing gains by being able to export 747s to the world market, with the increased output resulting in lower costs per plane and higher profits. The gains from such trade accrue not only to the exporting firm and country, but also to importing countries: they acquire 747s much more cheaply than they would be able to make them, at small volume, at home. Indeed, for any but the very largest countries, it would be out of the question to produce large commercial aircraft for the domestic market alone. It is of course true that large commercial aircraft are exceptional—the three firms dominating the world market produce at an output where their per unit costs are still falling significantly. Nevertheless, substantial economies of scale exist in many manufacturing processes. There are gains to be made from international specialization, even for countries whose economic fundamentals—in terms of climate, technology, resource endowments, and so forth—are very similar. A major feature of the international economy is the large volume of trade among the industrial countries; prosperous countries are the best customers of one another. The economies of scale to be reaped in the export market are one significant reason.

In the presence of economies of scale, firms have an incentive to expand; oligopolistic or monopolistic markets can result, with large firms having some price-setting power. Analytic complexities are introduced both by economies of scale themselves, and by the resulting concentration of market power. When these complexities are taken into account, the estimation of the effects of tariff reductions becomes a complicated and messy exercise. As a result, the older, simpler framework—with constant returns to scale and perfectly competitive markets—has remained very popular among international economists. Before looking at the effects of economies of scale, we will briefly review the results from models that assume constant returns.

CONSTANT RETURNS TO SCALE

Within this simple constant-returns, perfectly competitive framework, the standard tools of demand and supply can be applied to estimate the effects of a change in tariff rates. Consider, first, the effects of a reduction in our own tariffs. There are both gainers and losers in our domestic economy. The losers are the producers who compete with imported goods: as tariffs are cut and the prices of imports fall, domestic producers find it more difficult to compete. However, consumers gain; they can buy at lower prices. Finally, the government generally loses; it generally collects less tariff revenue as tariffs are reduced. Clearly, if tariffs are cut all the way to zero—as happens with free trade—then the government no longer collects any tariff revenues. By summing up the various gains and losses, the overall effects of a tariff cut can be estimated. In the annex to this chapter, demand and supply curves are used to illustrate the various gains and losses, together with the net "triangular" efficiency gains that generally result from a cut in tariffs.

Of course, the move to free trade requires the elimination not only of our own trade barriers, but also those of our trading partner (or partners). When our partner reduces its tariffs and other trade barriers, there is no need to balance gains and losses: we are the clear gainers from such a tariff reduction.[1] We can export more, and generally at higher prices, when foreign trade barriers are reduced. Indeed, this might be put forward as the first law of commercial policy: each country wants every other country to reduce its trade barriers. (The annex illustrates the gains when trading partners reduce their tariffs.)

Because trade between the two countries is so much more important to Canada than to the United States, most—though not all—of the empirical work on the effects of tariff reduction has been done in Canada. First, consider the simplest case: what would happen in the event of a *unilateral* elimination of tariffs by Canada. The effects of such an action were estimated about a decade ago (1978) by Robin Boadway (of Queen's University) and John Treddenick (of the Royal Military College of Canada). They concluded that Canadian real income would be depressed by a unilateral elimination of Canadian tariffs; that is, Canadian tariffs provide Canada with a small net benefit (less than 1 percent of GNP). The reason is that Canadian tariffs depress

---

1. There is an exception to this general proposition. A reduction of a foreign tariff on a primary or intermediate product may increase the effective protection on final products, with adverse effects on our exports of those products. For example, the reduction of foreign tariffs on computer chips will reduce the costs of foreign computer makers and make it easier for them to compete with our computer exports.

the prices received by firms exporting to Canada; thus, foreign exporters—rather than Canadian consumers—bear part of the burden of the Canadian tariff. In the Boadway-Treddenick study, the amount of the Canadian tariff paid by foreign producers more than outweighs any efficiency cost of the Canadian tariff; thus, Canada gains from its tariff and would suffer a small loss if it were removed unilaterally. More favorable results were found by Richard Harris (1984, p. 1028). He estimated that unilateral free trade would have little or no net effect on Canadian real incomes. That is, the amount of the Canadian tariff paid by foreign producers is approximately the same as the efficiency cost of the Canadian tariff.[2]

Such estimates of the effects of a unilateral tariff reduction (UTR) are, however, much less interesting than the effects of a *bilateral* (or multilateral) reduction. After all, countries generally do not reduce tariffs unilaterally, especially if they can persuade their trading partners to engage in a mutual reduction. Indeed, even a mutual reduction may become possible only if the desire of exporters for lower foreign barriers counterbalances the desire of import-competing industries for continued protection. Because producer interest tends to be concentrated, while the interests of consumers are diffuse and nebulous, the interests of exporting industries may provide a much more potent political force for trade liberalization than does the desire of domestic consumers for lower home tariffs and lower import prices.

In one study of bilateral free trade between the United States and Canada, Bob Hamilton and John Whalley of the University of Western Ontario (1985, p. 449) estimate that Canada would have received gains of US$1.3 billion if free trade had existed in the base year of 1977 (0.7 percent of GNP). For the United States, gains would have been $0.6 billion (0.03 percent of GNP).

Although they use a somewhat similar model (with constant returns to scale and perfectly competitive markets), Drusilla Brown of Tufts University and Robert Stern of the University of Michigan (1987) nevertheless come to a quite different conclusion—the United States, not Canada, would reap the greater gain from bilateral free trade. Indeed, their results suggest that, while the United States would gain

---

2. This result of Harris depends on an assumption of constant returns to scale. When economies of scale were introduced, Harris found that unilateral free trade would increase real income in Canada.

0.04 percent of GNP, Canada would lose about the same amount absolutely (or 0.4 percent of Canadian GNP), leaving no overall gain to the two countries.

What can possibly account for such a sharp difference in results, with the United States getting only a third of the gain in the Hamilton-Whalley study, while being the only gainer in the Brown-Stern study? The principal reason is that two quite different factors are at work, one favoring the United States and the other favoring Canada. The United States tends to gain from bilateral free trade because Canada would be dismantling its higher barriers to trade: Canadian tariff rates are generally higher than those of the United States (table 1.1), and they apply to a larger fraction of trade. This difference in existing tariffs dominates the Brown-Stern study, with the result that the United States is the only gainer. (Canada loses because its terms of trade worsen.)

On the other hand, Hamilton and Whalley attribute their conclusion—that Canada reaps the larger gain—to the fact that the Canadian market is so much smaller than that of the United States. Because the domestic US market is so large, it has the predominant influence over prices. As a result, the burden of *both* tariffs falls mainly on Canada. The Canadian tariff results primarily in a rise in the prices paid by Canadian consumers; its effect in depressing the prices received by US exporters is generally less strong. On the other side, the US tariff falls primarily on Canadian exporters. To sell in the very competitive US market, Canadian exporters generally have to absorb most of the US tariff; they cannot pass very much of it along to their customers. Accordingly, a bilateral abolition of tariffs would benefit Canadian consumers (as a group), since they would pay less for imports, and would also benefit Canadian producers (as a group), since they would be able to sell duty-free in the US market. Thus, Canada has a particularly strong stake in bilateral free trade.

These differing results should warn us against jumping to conclusions.[3] Nevertheless, existing empirical work suggests that, *if economies of scale and market imperfections are ruled out*, then:

• The division of gains between the two countries is uncertain. The fact that Canada has the smaller market tends to make it the larger

---

3. For additional information on empirical studies, see the surveys in Brown and Stern (1987) and Hill and Whalley (1985).

gainer (Hamilton-Whalley). But gains would tend to be thrown toward the United States because Canada would be cutting its higher tariffs (Brown-Stern).

• Gains from bilateral free trade between the United States and Canada would be quite small for each country, almost certainly less than 1 percent of GNP.

The second conclusion—that triangular welfare gains from trade liberalization are small—is consistent with other empirical studies that assume constant returns to scale. Whether for North America or other areas, estimates of the efficiency costs of protection are almost universally less than 1 percent of GNP, often much less. This has led to some discomfort on the part of international economists—if the efficiency triangles are so small, then perhaps the whole topic of commercial policy is trivial, at least as far as the overall performance of the economy is concerned. (Of course, individual exporting and import-competing firms may have an intense interest in commercial policy, even if the net effect of a tariff amounts to much less than 1 percent of GNP.)

ECONOMIES OF SCALE

Once economies of scale are introduced, however, the amounts at stake from changes in commercial policy can become much larger— they can become substantial blocks, rather than small triangles.[4]

---

4. Economies of scale introduce an important paradox into international trade theory. On the one hand, they undercut the neat theoretical case that exists for free trade in a world of constant returns to scale and perfect competition. In such a world, prices equal marginal costs; the free market provides an efficient solution (provided that externalities such as pollution are ruled out). Once economies of scale and imperfect markets are introduced, marginal cost is generally less than price, and the free-market solution is no longer optimal. Indeed, one of the cornerstones of protection is the infant-industry argument, which is based in part on economies of scale.

Paradoxically, however, economies of scale greatly strengthen the case for free trade, at least from the collective international perspective. Most obviously, it is a mistake to split up production in many small national units, if there are major efficiencies from large-scale production.

In brief, economies of scale may increase the incentives for an individual country to adopt protectionist policies. But they can greatly increase the general gain from a multilateral international agreement to reduce trade barriers. The relationship between economies of scale and trade theory and policy is one of the most important, though least understood, aspects of international economics.

FIGURE 2.1   **Costs and market size**

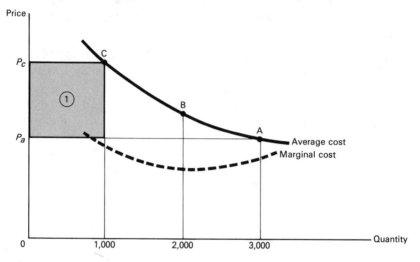

This is illustrated in figure 2.1, where average total cost falls over an extended range because of economies of scale. In a large domestic economy, such as the United States, there generally are strong competitive pressures to expand quickly to a point such as A, where per unit cost is at or close to the minimum. Failure to do so is to remain a high-cost producer, and risk elimination by large, low-cost competitors. However, even in the United States, some markets may be too small to support even one producer at a low-cost point such as A. We have already referred to the case of Boeing, where even the whole world market is not large enough to support production at A. Boeing can survive quite nicely at B, a point where per unit costs are still falling significantly, because the market is simply not large enough for any competitor to reach a point such as A.

Where the domestic market is too small to support efficient-scale producers—as is the case in some markets in the United States and many markets in Canada—very large gains can come from international trade. For example, consider a Canadian manufacturer, making three different products, at small scale (for example, at a point like C) for the domestic market, protected from import competition by a tariff wall. In the event of bilateral free trade—that is, the elimination of trade barriers by both the United States and Canada—the Canadian

producer will be faced with both a major danger and a major opportunity. The danger will come from the competition from high volume
producers in the United States. Even if US firms have to pay somewhat
higher wages, they will have the advantages of scale economies, and
will be able to undercut the Canadian producer at C. For the Canadian
manufacturer, doing things the old way would be suicidal. But access
to the large US market will provide a major opportunity. By cutting
back on his product line and concentrating on a single item, the
Canadian manufacturer will be able to move down along the cost
function toward A, selling much of his product in the United States.

In this case, the gains from free trade can be very large indeed.
Without detailed information on market conditions and the broader
economic adjustments occurring at the same time (including exchange
rate changes), it is not possible to say how this gain will be divided
among the consumer (in terms of lower prices), the business (in terms
of higher profits), and workers (in terms of higher wages). However,
the magnitude of the gains can be illustrated in the simple case where
producers price at their average cost (including normal profits). In this
case, Canadian consumers will be able to buy the product at P_a rather
than P_c, resulting in a gain of rectangular area 1. (They will also gain
a triangular area—not shown here—on their additional purchases when
the price falls.) In addition, they will be able to reap similar, large
rectangular gains on the other two products being imported at low
prices from the United States. And, unlike the situation in the previous
section, *this gain to the consumer does not come at the expense of
the producer:* the producer can afford to sell at the lower price, without
any reduction in profitability, because economies of scale are lowering
per unit costs.

EMPIRICAL ESTIMATES WITH ECONOMIES OF SCALE

When economies of scale are taken into account, not only does the
potential for gain become much larger than with constant returns. In
addition, Canada is likely to reap most of the gain.[5]

5. This is the conclusion reached in most studies, but not by everyone. Wigle (1986,
p. 16), is an exception. Using a model with economies of scale and imperfect competition,
he comes to conclusions similar to those of Brown and Stern. Because Canada has
higher tariffs, he estimates that the terms of trade would move in favor of the United
States with bilateral free trade. The United States would consequently capture all, or
almost all, the efficiency gains. (Canada might either gain or lose, with Wigle's best
estimate being a small loss.)

For the past twenty-five years, Canadian economists have been fascinated by a major difference between the way many manufacturing operations are conducted in the United States and Canada.[6] Particularly in the manufacturing of consumer durables, there has been a tendency for Canadian manufacturers to produce a wide range of products, each in a relatively small quantity.

The standard explanation for this is that diversified, small-scale production is encouraged by the trade barriers of *both* Canada and its trading partners—particularly its most important partner, the United States. The Canadian tariff and other trade barriers provide a protected, high-priced market, making it profitable to produce a wide variety of products, even if they are expensive by international standards. The US tariff and other trade barriers encourage Canadian producers to focus on the small Canadian market by limiting their access to the large market to the south. A further incentive to fragmented, short production runs in Canada is the exposure of the Canadian public to US advertising, which reinforces the desire of consumers for choice among a wide range of products.

Concern with the inefficiencies caused by small-scale production has been a driving force behind Canadian commercial policy in the past two decades. It was a major reason for the automotive agreement between Canada and the United States in 1965, which permits duty-free passage of automobiles and original equipment parts between the two countries, and thus permits specialization by the Canadian subsidiaries of US auto companies (chapter 4). They now produce for the combined US-Canadian market, exporting much of their output, while much of the Canadian market is satisfied from US factories.

Two decades ago, the present author was involved in a research project to quantify the potential gains from bilateral free trade between the United States and Canada. We concluded (Wonnacott and Wonnacott 1967, p. 300) that a mutual elimination of trade barriers would allow Canadian industry to produce at a much more efficient scale. After a period of adjustment, bilateral free trade would contribute

---

6. For example, Baldwin and Gorecki (1986), Eastman and Stykolt (1967), English (1964), Harris and Cox (1984), and Wonnacott and Wonnacott (1967). See also Spence (1977).

between 7 percent and 10.5 percent to real GNP in Canada. Because of trade liberalization since our study—including the Auto Pact—gains would now be somewhat smaller (Wonnacott and Wonnacott 1982).

More recently, Richard Harris (of Queen's University) and David Cox (of the University of Western Ontario) have presented a much more formal analysis (1984). They have developed a major general equilibrium model in which firms enjoy economies of scale. Because economies of scale at the firm level are inconsistent with perfect competition, Harris and Cox also assume imperfectly competitive product markets, with some collusive behavior among sellers.

In this model, even a *unilateral* reduction in tariffs by Canada would have a significant effect on Canadian industrial organization, efficiency, and national income. Cox and Harris (1985, table 1) estimate a unilateral reduction of Canadian tariffs in 1976 would have led to an increase of about 3.5 percent of Canadian GNP, as the market power of Canadian manufacturing industries was sharply reduced and they were encouraged to specialize in longer production runs.

Again, however, it is a *bilateral* reduction in tariffs that would provide the larger gain. In more recent work, based on data for the early 1980s, Harris (1985, p. 173) concluded that Canadian real GNP would have been increased by 9 percent by a free trade agreement between the United States and Canada. (The figure would be smaller now because of tariff cuts since 1980.) Indeed, Harris found that Canada would have slightly more to gain from a bilateral free trade agreement than from *multilateral* free trade; the privilege of duty-free entry into the US market, when overseas competitors would still face US trade barriers, would be a more important source of gain to Canadian suppliers than a broader, multilateral move to free trade.

The Harris-Cox research has attracted wide attention; in the words of John Whalley (1984, p. 387), it is "undoubtedly one of the most important pieces of applied research to be done on a Canadian policy issue for many a year." Its high estimate of the gains from trade liberalization has been one of the reasons for the renewed Canadian interest in bilateral negotiations with the United States. Its methodological innovations—introducing scale economies and imperfect competition into a general-equilibrium framework—promise to open up a major new field of economic research.

This type of work is extraordinarily difficult, and the Harris-Cox (HC) results have quite properly been subject to critical review. One problem is that their results depend very much on the estimates of economies of scale. HC do not make independent estimates of scale economies; they rely on previous econometric work and engineering studies. One difficulty is that there are outstanding, unsettled econometric problems in estimating economies of scale statistically, which mean that estimates may be inaccurate. The higher engineering estimates do not provide reassurance, because they may be subject to an upward bias, particularly because of the difficulty of disentangling variable and overhead costs. To the degree that the estimates of economies of scale are in fact biased in an upward direction, the actual gains from trade liberalization would be smaller than suggested by Harris and Cox. Nevertheless, Harris and Cox have provided substantial support to earlier, less formal work which suggested that economies of scale would be a key source of gain in the event of trade liberalization.

Further support of the idea that tariffs are an important reason for short, inefficient production runs in Canada has been provided by the recent work by Baldwin and Gorecki (1986), using a comprehensive Statistics Canada data set covering 167 manufacturing industries. They find that industries with high tariffs and high concentration have shorter production runs and greater product diversity than elsewhere in the manufacturing sector. Furthermore, they find that the larger Canadian plants were small compared to larger US plants, but that Canadian plant size increased by about one-third between 1970 and 1979 when signficant tariff cuts were occurring. In addition, the length of production runs increased as tariffs were being reduced, and product diversity within plants decreased (1983a, b, c). (However, these changes are not necessarily due to tariff cuts; they might also be the result of technological change occurring at the same time.) Trade liberalization causes the rationalization, rather than the disappearance of Canadian industries. Baldwin and Gorecki conclude (1986, p. 171):

A strong argument can be made that the trade liberalization process over the postwar period has improved the competitiveness of Canadian industry and that continued emphasis on a reduction of trade barriers or their maintenance at present low levels is in Canada's best interests.

Intraindustry and Interindustry Adjustment

Reductions in trade barriers generally improve long-run economic efficiency, but they can cause dislocations and require adjustments. With a broad bilateral free trade arrangement, two types of adjustment would occur:

• adjustment *within* industries, particularly in Canada, as plants and firms specialize for the larger North American market

• adjustment *between* industries, as the United States tends to specialize in some products and Canada in others.

Because the trade barriers of both countries have encouraged short-run, fragmented production processes in Canada, the first type would be an important part of the overall adjustment process. Free trade would provide an incentive to cut back on the diversity of products, and make fewer goods at larger scale. This type of adjustment would present a major challenge for management: firms and plants would have to be reorganized, and specialization increased. However, this would be relatively painless: adjustments within industries—and even more so within plants—are less disruptive than those between industries, where workers may be required to adjust either by acquiring new skills or moving in order to find alternative employment. Nevertheless, even adjustments within industries can cause pain. For example, the Canadian furniture industry is one where substantial adjustment may have to take place. Not only is production fragmented among various lines and styles of goods, but the average size of plant is small by international standards. Some plants will have to close, and consolidation take place.

Although much of the overall adjustment would be of the less painful, intraindustry type, there would nonetheless also be some adjustment between industries. Because free trade would open up larger markets and make possible longer production runs, it would help some firms reduce their costs. Consequently, current costs and selling prices cannot be taken as a clear signal of which industries would expand, and which would contract in the event of free trade.

Nevertheless, some work has been done on the question of interindustry adjustment. The results are summarized in table 2.1. The first

TABLE 2.1 Sectoral effects of bilateral free trade

	(1)	(2) Brown-	(3)	(4) Royal	(5)
Study by:	Harris	Stern	Magun	Commission	USTR
Aluminum products					Y
Chemicals	*	U	(U)		
Construction		(U)	*		
Consumer products				U	
Home appliances					Y
Cosmetics					Y
Electrical equipment	*	U		U	Y
Electronics				U	
Financial services		U	*		
Food and beverages	*e	(U)	*		
Footwear		*		U	
Forestry products		(C)		C	
Paper (and paper products)	(C)	*	*	C	
Furniture	(U)	*	(U)	U	Y
Informatics					Y
Nonferrous metals		(C)			
Leather	*e	*	}U{		Y
Leather products					N
Machinery				U	
Machinery equipment			C		
Agricultural equipment	(U)				Y
Nonagricultural equipment	(U)				
Metal fabrication	*e	U	*		

Note: The symbols represent the following:

Harris (column 1):
- C   if predicted Canadian production up 200 percent
- (C) if Canadian production up 25 percent to 200 percent
- (U) if Canadian production down 10 percent to 20 percent
- U   if Canadian production down more than 20 percent
- e   if Canadian employment down in spite of increase in Canadian production
- *   if Canadian production effects less than specified above (that is, an increase of less than 25 percent or decrease of less than 10 percent)

Brown-Stern (column 2):
- C   if predicted Canadian production up at least US$100 million, and US output down at least $50 million
- (C) if Canadian production up at least US$30 million, and US production down at least $15 million
- (U) if US production up at least US$30 million, and Canadian production down at least $15 million
- U   if US production up at least US$100 million, and Canadian production down at least $50 million
- *   if production effects less than specified above (that is, an increase of less than $30 million, decrease of less than $15 million)

Study by:	(1) Harris	(2) Brown- Stern	(3) Magun	(4) Royal Commission	(5) USTR
Petroleum	*e				
Petroleum products		C			
Printing	*	(U)	*		Y
Rubber	(C)	*			
Rubber and plastic products			(U)		
Scientific equipment				U	
Steel and iron		*			
Steel	*e				
Carbon					N
Fabricated structural					Y
Textiles	C	(U)	(U)	U	N
Clothing	C	*	(U)	U	N
Knitting	(C)		U		
Wool	*e				
Tires				U	
Tobacco	(C)e		*		
Transportation		(U)			
Transportation and storage			(C)		
Urban transportation equipment	(C)	}C{	(C)	C	N
Transport equipment	(C)				
Wholesale trade		U	(C)		
Miscellaneous manufacturing (coverage varies)	(U)	*	U		

Magun (column 3):
  C   if predicted Canadian production up at least 10 percent
  (C) if Canadian production up 2.5 percent to 10 percent
  (U) if Canadian production down 2.5 percent to 10 percent
  U   if Canadian production down at least 10 percent
  *   if Canadian production effects less than specified above (that is, a change of less than 2.5 percent)

Royal Commission on the Economic Union and Development Prospects for Canada (column 4):
  C for industries of Canadian strength
  U for industries of Canadian weakness

US Trade Representative (column 5):
  Y where US industry urged bilateral sectoral negotiation
  N where US industry opposed bilateral sectoral negotiation

Sources: Harris (1985), p. 176; Brown and Stern (1987), table 5; Magun (1986), table 2; Royal Commission on the Economic Union and Development Prospects for Canada (1985), vol. 1, pp. 343–48; Hufbauer and Samet (1985), p. 185 (summary of industry responses to US Trade Representative).

column shows the interindustry adjustment projected by Harris (1985), with C representing industries where substantial increases in output (200 percent or more) would occur in Canada with free trade, and (C) representing industries of less strong Canadian advantage. Similarly, U and (U) represent industries of US advantage.[7] Because Harris was using a model with economies of scale, an increase in output could in some cases occur with fewer workers. The letter e represents such industries, where the rationalization of the Canadian industry was predicted to cause a fall in employment, even as output was increasing.

The next two columns summarize the results from studies assuming constant returns to scale—Brown-Stern (column 2), and a 1986 study by Sunder Magun of the Economic Council of Canada, using the input-output model of the University of Maryland (column 3).[8] Finally, the last two columns come from less formal sources. In column 4, C represents industries identified as sectors of Canadian strength by the Royal Commission on the Economic Union and Development Prospects for Canada, while U represents the sectors of Canadian weakness and US strength. Column 5 reports the "yes" or "no" responses of US industries to the US Trade Representative, when asked about the desirability of negotiations for sectoral free trade. Although sector-by-sector free trade agreements would have different effects from a comprehensive agreement, a Y (yes) answer suggests this is an industry of perceived US strength, and N an industry of US weakness.

A number of industries stand out as candidates for US expansion and Canadian contraction—most clearly furniture, but also chemicals, electrical equipment, and miscellaneous manufacturing. On the other side, Canadian strength was identified in forestry products, paper, and urban transportation equipment.

---

7. Harris focused on what would happen to Canadian industry, and made no independent estimate of changes in output in the United States. The industries shown as ones of US advantage in column 1, table 2.1, are those where Harris predicted that Canadian output would fall.

8. In the models with constant returns, the effect of free trade on total output is much smaller than in models with increasing returns. Consequently, the cutoff numbers chosen for C, (C), U and (U) are smaller in column 3 than column 1. In models with constant returns, employment is closely proportional to changes in output; hence, there is no need to identify employment changes (e) separately in columns 2 and 3. Details on cutoff points are provided in the footnote to table 2.1.

Regarding the vulnerable Canadian *furniture* industry, the Royal Commission (1985, pp. 345–46) provided a number of insights. The Canadian office-furniture industry would be in a relatively good position in a North American Free Trade Association (NAFTA). However, the household furniture industry would face more intense competitive pressures, and it might have some difficulty in responding. The industry is fragmented, operating in many small plants which cannot all expand to efficient rates of production. The outlook is not entirely bleak, however. One Canadian firm is already operating at a relatively large rate of output, and exporting a significant portion of its output. All in all, the furniture industry is a case where the disadvantages of operating in the small Canadian market have been particularly acute. Consumers naturally want diversity and a choice of style. But the Canadian market is just too small to permit the efficient production of a wide variety of goods. The consumer ends up paying a high price for the luxury of choice in this high-tariff industry (with protection of 14 percent).[9]

Even in the areas of potential Canadian strength, substantial changes might be required to take advantage of the potential. This is most notably the case in *paper*. Although access to raw materials provides a major advantage, Canadian paper-making machinery is outdated. The Royal Commission reports (1985, p. 343) that about half the paper-making machines in Canada were made before 1950, compared to about 25 percent in the United States and only 5 percent in Scandinavia.

Of the industries of Canadian strength, two raise special problems in negotiations between the United States and Canada—namely, forest products and urban transportation equipment. The *lumber* industry has recently been the subject of a countervailing duty procedure in the United States; details will be provided in chapter 4. *Urban transportation equipment* depends on government procurement procedures; "Buy America" provisions in the United States have been a barrier to Canadian sales (chapter 5). These two industries illustrate why Canada (as well as the United States) is eager that any agreement go beyond an elimination of tariffs, and deal with other barriers to commerce.

In table 2.1, perhaps the most interesting industries are *textiles* and

---

9. For earlier work on the furniture industry, providing much more detail, see Bond and Wonnacott (1968).

clothing, because of the conflicting suggestions on where the advantage lies between the United States and Canada. The studies that assumed constant returns (columns 2 and 3) identified them as areas of US strength, and so did the Royal Commission. But the US industry apparently fears bilateral free trade; it wanted nothing to do with negotiations (column 5).[10] And Harris identified textiles and clothing as sectors of potential Canadian strength. (Indeed, his results indicated an expansion of Canadian output of more than 100 percent in knitting, more than 200 percent in textiles, and more than 400 percent in clothing.) These apparently contradictory results might possibly be explained along the following lines. The contrast between the constant returns and increasing returns suggests that these would be sectors where internal reorganization of Canadian industry would be particularly important, to meet the competitive conditions of a large, integrated North American market. The negative views picked up by officials in both countries (columns 4 and 5) may reflect a sense of insecurity and turbulence within the industries on both sides of the border, which might be explained by the intensity of competition from *overseas* suppliers. While US and Canadian industries are both under pressure from overseas, it would not, of course, be possible for each of them to lose market shares to the other in a bilateral free trade area (although some industrial subsectors might tend to migrate to the United States and others to Canada). Indeed, insofar as a North American Free Trade Association permitted a rationalization of the North American industries, it would increase their ability to meet competition from overseas. (NAFTA should not, however, be seen as a panacea: the industries in both countries are likely to remain subject to intense

---

10. The negative view on the bilateral talks was reiterated in the Statement of the American Textile Manufacturers Association (ATMA) to the US International Trade Commission (1986). In that document (p. 2), the ATMA based its case heavily on the argument that trade would inevitably flow strongly in Canada's favor, because of the difference in size of the two markets: "The mere fact that an FTA would grant Canada unencumbered access to a market ten times larger than the one we would gain access to means that the United States cannot possibly achieve equity and parity under such an arrangement." This argument does not seem to be valid; as a free trade association is formed, there is no strong tendency for the trade balance of smaller members to improve (for example, the Netherlands or Luxemburg in the initial European Community, or Greece more recently). Within the free trade association represented by the United States, the smaller states have no clear advantage over the larger ones.

overseas competition, regardless of any bilateral trading agreement between Canada and the United States.)

Finally, something should be said about the *steel* industry, where the two countries have entered a "gentlemen's agreement" to limit Canadian exports. As with many informal agreements, there is some difference of opinion as to just what has been agreed upon, but, at the least, Canada has agreed not to increase its share of the US market; that is, it is not to take advantage of US restraints on imports from other countries. This agreement, and the preceding increases in Canadian steel exports to the United States, have contributed to the common view that the US industry is vulnerable to competition from Canada, with bilateral free trade likely leading to a substantial penetration of the US market by Canadian firms. However, this view does not find support in table 2.1. The Brown-Stern and Harris studies each find relatively small effects of bilateral free trade. Brown and Stern find that there would be some expansion in the iron and steel industry in *each* country, rather than a net migration from one country to the other. (This apparently is a result of an improved strength to meet overseas competition.) Harris—who does not estimate changes in output in the United States—foresees an increase of 21 percent in Canadian steel production, or less than the average increase in overall industrial production in Canada. (Increases in Canadian production are large in the Harris model because he includes economies of scale.) Furthermore, Harris foresees a small decrease in Canadian employment. (More can be produced with fewer workers, because of the greater efficiencies.) In sum, the empirical work does not support the view that free trade would lead Canada to capture a substantially larger share of the North American steel market at the expense of US steel.

Robert Crandall of the Brookings Institution (1987) has suggested some of the pieces that might help solve the steel industry puzzle. The traditional steel-producing areas of the United States have been under severe pressure in recent years, not only because of imports, but also because steel usage has fallen far short of what was expected a decade ago. In 1975, the American Iron and Steel Institute forecast raw steel production of 170 million tons in 1983; actual production was only 85 million tons. At about 20 percent of the market, imports have added significantly to the difficulties of the steel industry, but they account for only a fraction of the huge shortfall from anticipated production. The soft US market for steel has also changed the relationship between new production and the supply of scrap, causing downward pressure on scrap prices. This has made electric-furnace melting of scrap attractive, and added to the growth of minimill production relative to that of the large integrated firms. In brief, the traditional steel-producing areas have faced a combination of problems. Not only has the overall market fallen far short of forecasts, but the traditional integrated producers have seen their share fall to about 65 percent of the US market, with roughly 20 percent going to imports and 15 percent to minimills. Crandall suggests that this trend will continue. He forecasts that, by the year 2000, integrated US production will fall to 50 percent of the US market, with imports and US minimills each taking about 25 percent.

In recent years, the Canadian companies generally have been healthier than the integrated US steel companies. Although Stelco's new Nanticoke plant and Dofasco's Hamilton expansion have been rather successful, Crandall does not attribute Canadian success to higher investment. Between 1976 and 1982, Canadian investment in steelmaking, measured in US dollars per ton of steel actually shipped, was very close to that in the United States. In 1983 and 1984, Canadian investment dropped sharply, to only a third the rate in the United States (again with investment measured as dollars per ton of steel shipped). Within the United States, Crandall finds that the firms with the highest rate of reinvestment have generally been the *least* successful—a not entirely surprising result in an industry where the market has fallen so far short of forecasts.

One reason for the relative success of the Canadian industry has been lower wages. However, since 1982, the hourly compensation of US labor in the steel industry has declined, following an increase of more than 300 percent between 1970 and 1982. Between 1982 and 1984, Canadian hourly compensation rose from 65 percent of the US rate to 77 percent. Crandall doubts that the more successful performance of the Canadian steel industry will continue. The US industry should be less vulnerable to major Canadian inroads than in the past. Nevertheless, because of slack demand and competition from overseas and minimills, the old steel-producing areas are likely to face continuing economic and political problems—regardless of what happens to bilateral trade between the United States and Canada.

Effects on the United States

For the United States, the same three broad issues arise as for Canada:

- the size of triangular efficiency effects

- gains from the greater exploitation of economies of scale

- the amount of interindustry adjustment.

In addition, a number of other issues should be taken into account when judging the effects on the United States:

- the implications for US-owned firms in Canada

- the effect that a bilateral arrangement may have on US relations with other countries, and the operation of the overall international economic system. This issue arises for any country considering a regional free trade agreement, but is particularly significant for the United States, with its traditional emphasis on multilateral negotiations and the most-favored-nation principle.

We have just considered intraindustry adjustment. We now turn to the other items.

TRIANGULAR EFFICIENCY EFFECTS

Earlier, we noted two estimates of the triangular efficiency gains to the United States in models assuming constant returns to scale—those of Brown-Stern (0.03 percent of US GNP), and Hamilton-Whalley (0.04 percent). The two studies are in close agreement: because the US market is so much larger, the results are less responsive to changes in assumption than is the case for Canada. In an area of research where it is difficult to come to firm conclusions, this is one result in which we may place a high degree of confidence: there are triangular gains for the United States, but they are almost certainly a small fraction of 1 percent of GNP.

ECONOMIES OF SCALE

We may also be confident about a second conclusion—the potential for gain from economies of scale is certainly less for the United States than Canada, both absolutely, and, *a fortiori*, as a percentage of GNP. The reasons are quite straightforward. The large US market already provides great scope for the exploitation of economies of scale. And access to the Canadian market—which is only about one-tenth the size of the US market—would provide little additional scope for the lengthening of production runs for the typical US business.

Nevertheless, there would be some gains, particularly for US firms in areas near the Canadian border that will benefit from improved access to the Canadian market—a market roughly the size of the section of the United States from Milwaukee to the northern border of California. Although access to the Canadian market would not make a great difference to the average US firm, it could be quite important for specialized firms occupying market niches. This type of gain—to smaller, specialized firms—is not picked up in the comprehensive economic models, which must of necessity deal with major industries.

Furthermore, there would be another source of gain to US businesses: insofar as free trade contributed to a major expansion of the Canadian economy and an increase in Canadian incomes, Canada would be in a position to buy more US exports. The best foreign market for US exports would become even better.[11]

In addition to providing the opportunity to add low-cost, long production lines, the increase in the size of the market open to both US and Canadian producers would contribute to the performance of both economies in several interrelated ways:

• A broader North American trading arrangement would help to ease the *antitrust dilemma*. One problem with restricting the size of firms by antitrust action is that it may reduce their ability to compete on world markets. The larger the market to which firms have unimpeded access, the more it is possible to have the advantages both of large firms and of competitive market conditions.

• A related advantage is that an integration of the North American market would provide a larger *home base*, and thus enhance the ability of firms (both US and Canadian) to export into the increasingly

---

11. This point is emphasized by Peter Morici (1987), in a section entitled "What the Models Don't Tell Us."

competitive world market. It would also enhance their ability to compete in their home markets with imports from overseas nations.

However, the amounts at stake are smaller for the United States than Canada. If a free trade arrangement were phased in over a number of years—as seems likely—many of the effects on US industry would be hard to identify even after the fact, because they would be lost in the major dynamic changes taking place continuously. Nevertheless, larger markets should contribute to greater economies of scale, and make it possible to combine large-scale business and a competitive economy.

DIVISION OF GAINS: IS FAIRNESS AN ISSUE?

When economies of scale are taken into account, we have seen that the larger gains from a free trade arrangement would go to Canada. This raises the question: would a free trade agreement therefore be unfair? Does fairness require a 50-50 split of the gains? The answer is no. There is no particular reason to use an even split as a base line for judging fairness in an international agreement; the United States is not facing a bad deal if it reaps a smaller gain than Canada.

To see why this is so, it is perhaps helpful to divorce ourselves from the details of our actual international relations, and consider a fanciful historical "might-have-been." Suppose that, through a quirk of history or shortcoming of statesmanship, Maryland had been excluded from the United States, with exports from Maryland being subject to the tariffs of the remaining United States, and US exports to Maryland likewise being subject to Maryland tariffs. Without getting into the details of the markets for oysters, turtle soup, Appalachian coal, and corn, it is clear that the most notable effect of Maryland's exclusion would be to depress real incomes in Maryland, not the remaining 49 states. In other words, in the free trade arrangement between Maryland and the rest of the United States, most of the gain goes to Maryland. But that does not mean that Maryland gains an unfair advantage in its trade with the rest of the country. Indeed, any other state might have been excluded instead of Maryland: the same proposition would hold for each. One would scarcely argue that each state gains an unfair advantage in its trade with the other 49. Unevenness of the gains is the probable result when a small unit engages in open commerce with a larger unit. It is a characteristic of how markets work, not evidence of an unfair outcome. The key question for the larger community is not whether the gains are equal, but whether the net effects are positive—that is, whether the larger community gains rather than loses.

There is, however, an important message to be drawn from this comparison of the gains of the large and the small countries. In its relations with the larger neighbor, the smaller country is likely to feel an acute sense of vulnerability—it may be hurt severely by a breakdown in commercial relationships, even though the consequences may not be very great for the larger country. Indeed, one of the major reasons for the Canadian government to propose the current round of talks has been the widespread belief in Canada that protectionism is growing in the United States, and that it is important to reduce Canadian vulnerability by reaching an understanding with the United States over trade barriers.

FREE TRADE AND US SUBSIDIARIES IN CANADA

Free trade will promote a more efficient industry in Canada; this will be true both for Canadian-owned firms and the subsidiaries of US firms. This has been foreshadowed in the auto industry: the bilateral elimination of automotive tariffs in 1965 has led to a rationalization of the Canadian plants of GM, Ford, and Chrysler. They now produce fewer models, at greater volume.

It is reasonable to expect that a general increase in Canadian prosperity will also be shared by US subsidiaries, in the form of higher profits. (This will not invariably be the case, however. By increasing competition within the Canadian economy, a free trade arrangement may reduce monopoly or oligopoly profits of some firms.) US firms in Canada will also gain in terms of more predictable and stable conditions for doing business. For example, a free trade agreement should include an understanding on investment policies. While free trade does not require the right of establishment in all sectors (particularly in sensitive areas such as cultural enterprises), a trade agreement should prohibit some past Canadian requirements for firms setting up shop in Canada— for example, limits on their imports or target levels of exports (chapter

5). Although Canada has moved away from some policies that US firms found objectionable—for example, by relaxing requirements for foreign investors and by working toward an accommodation on pharmaceutical patents—the status quo is not necessarily stable. If the recent Canadian initiative for free trade is rebuffed, a return to the policies of the recent past—or even more nationalistic policies—is possible. If this happens, the subsidiaries of US firms are likely to suffer.

A Bilateral Agreement and the Most-Favored-Nation Principle

The most-favored-nation principle has been a cornerstone of US commercial policy since the 1920s, although there have been a number of exceptions, such as the historical ties to the Philippines, the bilateral US-Canadian automotive agreement of 1965, and the recent bilateral free trade agreement with Israel. When the rules of the GATT were established in the late 1940s, as part of the postwar international economic system, the MFN principle was a fundamental starting point (Article I).

Prior to the general commitment to MFN under the GATT, an MFN clause was included in trade agreements as a way of pinning our trading partners down, and gaining some assurance that they would, in fact, open their markets to us if we opened our markets to them. In the absence of the MFN clause, we might be quite uncertain that we would actually benefit if one of our trading partners agreed to reduce its duties on our products, for example, a reduction of the duty on our machines from 40 percent to 20 percent. The problem was that this country might turn around and negotiate an even lower duty—of, say, 10 percent—with the Germans, leaving US machinery exporters at a disadvantage. The MFN clause was designed to prevent such discrimination. If the other country cut its duty on German machinery to 10 percent, it was required to give us "most-favored-nation treatment," and cut the duty on our machinery to 10 percent, too.

In the period following World War II, the MFN principle became an important part of the trading system established through the GATT;

concessions granted to any country would be extended to all GATT members. The MFN has a number of advantages:

• It promotes economic efficiency (because it encourages purchases from the lowest-cost foreign producer, rather than from a country with whom a special, discriminatory deal has been negotiated).

• It reduces disputes over past agreements.

• It safeguards the interests of third countries when any two other countries negotiate.

The safeguarding of third-country interests was seen as a cornerstone in building a harmonious multilateral trading system.

The MFN principle is not, however, without its drawbacks, most notably the "free rider" problem. Once countries are assured that concessions will be extended to their exports, they may be inclined to sit back, let other countries negotiate lower tariffs, and obtain a "free ride" when these tariff reductions are extended to their exports. One way of dealing with this problem was to make trade negotiations as broad as possible; hence the various major "rounds" of GATT negotiations.

This solution, however, led to another difficulty—the "convoy" problem. Even while participating in multilateral negotiations, countries might hold back, agreeing only to minimal concessions. Other participants would then be faced with a choice: of being held back to the speed of the slowest ship in the convoy, or proceeding ahead at a faster pace, giving the laggards something of a free ride.

The free rider-convoy problem has become particularly troublesome as GATT negotiations have addressed new topics, where some members have been reluctant to negotiate. The result has been a *conditional* application of MFN. Thus, the Code on Subsidies and Countervailing Duties requires MFN treatment, but only for the subset of GATT countries actually agreeing to the code. A greater use of the conditional MFN approach has been suggested as a way of getting agreement in other nontariff areas (Hufbauer and Schott 1985, pp. 19–22) while maintaining an "unconditional" MFN approach for tariffs. (To be precise, the GATT requires only conditional MFN even for tariffs: MFN privileges need be extended only to *members* of GATT. This means that nonmembers cannot be assured of a free ride, and they are thereby encouraged to join GATT.)

The MFN principle has also been eroded in other ways. As tariffs have been lowered through successive GATT negotiations, nontariff barriers (NTBs) have grown in relative importance. By their very nature, NTBs give themselves to discriminatory application. Some nations may be favored over others when quotas are allocated. For example, quotas are generally based on historical shares, thus favoring traditional suppliers at the expense of new producers. Similarly, the "voluntary" export restraints discriminate, particularly against major suppliers.

Nevertheless, the MFN principle remains at the heart of the GATT system. If it is not applied, at least to tariffs, there will be very little left of the multilateral trading system established at the end of World War II. In entering negotiations with Canada over a free trade agreement, one question for the United States is how these negotiations are related to its overall trade strategy, and, in particular, with the MFN principle. Canada, too, has an interest in the maintenance of the multilateral GATT system. In his announcement that Canada wished to pursue a new trade agreement with the United States, Prime Minister Brian Mulroney (1985) explicitly declared that, "Any new agreement between Canada and the United States would have to meet the test of our over-riding obligations under the GATT." For this goal to be achieved, a US-Canadian agreement would have to meet GATT Article XXIV, setting out conditions for countries forming a customs union or free trade area.

ARTICLE XXIV

Article XXIV allows countries to grant one another special treatment by establishing a customs union (CU) or free trade area (FTA), provided that:

• Duties and other trade restrictions are "eliminated on substantially all the trade" among the participants;[12] that is, if the countries go all the way (or substantially all the way) to a complete customs union or free trade association (paragraph 8).

---

12. This point is qualified; barriers need be eliminated only on products *originating within* the association. That is, a FTA or CU is permitted to have origin rules, to restrict transshipment of imports from third countries. This qualification is considered in chapter 5.

• The elimination of internal barriers is scheduled to occur "within a reasonable length of time" (paragraph 5c). This is commonly interpreted as permitting a transition period of not more than 10 years.

• Duties and other barriers to imports from nonmember countries "shall not on the whole be higher or more restrictive" than those preceding the establishment of the customs union or FTA (paragraphs 5a, b). This provision was aimed at protecting the rights of third-country exporters.

The first provision may seem curious—to disapprove partial preferential arrangements covering only some products, while accepting broad arrangements covering (substantially) all products. It was supported on the ground that large, unrestricted markets provide substantial benefits—most notably, the internal market within the United States. Such benefits should also be available to others. For example, consideration was being given to an integration of the nations of Western Europe, for a combination of economic, political, and strategic reasons.

Shortly after Article XXIV was written, the economic effects of regional integration were addressed by Jacob Viner in his 1950 classic, *The Customs Union Issue*. As an economist, Viner saw efficiency as the main gain from international trade; trade encourages production in a less costly location. He posed a key question: would a customs union (or free trade association) improve economic efficiency or not? His short answer was: we can't be sure. A CU or FTA works to increase efficiency in one way, but to decrease it in another.

To explain why, Viner drew a distinction between two forces at work when a customs union is formed. As two (or more) countries cut tariffs on each other's products, *new trade* is *created*. Some goods previously bought from domestic producers are now purchased from the lower cost partner country. Such *trade creation* improves efficiency.

However, when we remove tariffs on our partner's goods, but not on the goods of outside countries, the partner now has preferred access to our market. As a result, we now *switch* some purchases, buying from our common market partner rather than from an outside country. Such *trade diversion* reduces efficiency; it represents a switch from an efficient source outside the customs union to a less efficient producer in the partner nation. A CU (or FTA) may be predominantly trade creating—in which it is economically desirable—or it may be predominantly trade diverting, in which case it is not.[13]

Viner's book thus introduced a skeptical note into the discussion of customs unions, which had previously been given broad approval without much detailed, critical analysis. Nevertheless, Viner's work supported the main points of Article XXIV. The prohibition against raising barriers to imports from outside countries not only protected third countries, but it also worked to limit the amount of trade diversion. Furthermore, the apparently curious provision—to disapprove partial preferential arrangements covering only some products, while accepting broad arrangements covering (substantially) all products—found support within Viner's framework. Because of the dynamics of trade negotiations, partial preferential arrangements tend to cause more trade diversion than trade creation.

SELECTIVE PREFERENCES

To see why, suppose that countries are permitted to get together to make whatever preferential agreements they wish. A natural way for a country to open negotiations would be something like the following: "Look, we're now importing computer chips from Japan, while you're importing TV sets from Hong Kong. We'll cut our tariffs on your chips—allowing you to take our market for chips away from the Japanese—if you will cut your tariffs on TVs, and thus allow us to come into your market and compete with those unfair, low-wage producers in Hong Kong." It is much less likely for countries to negotiate on products where the domestic industry is vulnerable, and where a preferential tariff cut would lead to new imports from the partner and a shrinkage of the domestic industry (in other words, on products where trade creation would occur).[14] Thus, if countries are

---

13. As has been pointed out by Lipsey (1957), Meade (1955), and a number of other writers, trade diversion does not *necessarily* lead to a decrease in efficiency in all cases. The extra costs of buying from a higher cost source may be offset, or more than offset, by triangular gains to consumers when the prices of imports fall as a result of the removal of tariffs.

14. Notice the difference in emphasis between the economist's approach and that of a business executive or politician. The economist takes into account the gain from cheap

allowed to pick and choose among products in a preferential arrangement, the negotiating process is likely to be biased, resulting mostly in trade diversion, and little if any trade creation. So goes the economic argument against selective preferences.

Recent work has reinforced the case for a comprehensive approach, covering "substantially all" goods. In a comprehensive arrangement, the efficiency gains in any one sector would have substantial effects on others (as emphasized, for example, by Harris 1985, p. 175). This means that the approach to Canadian-US trade tentatively considered several years ago—a gradual, sector-by-sector reduction of barriers—would involve continuing problems of adjustment and readjustment. Furthermore, if some industries are excluded from a free trade agreement, with continuing protection resulting in the persistence of high prices, then the users of such products will be at a competitive disadvantage in the North American market. Finally, once a process of exempting specific sectors is begun, there is a danger that a comprehensive trade deal might unravel.

Nevertheless, the negotiators of the two sides face a number of major difficulties (chapters 4 and 5). The question therefore arises as to what will happen if a comprehensive agreement becomes impossible. One option would be to cut back sharply, to negotiate an agreement on such issues as the treatment of intellectual property, services, the administration of customs procedures, principles for international investment, and the establishment of a mechanism for dealing with bilateral trade disputes. Agreement on such matters would raise no threat to the GATT system; indeed, bilateral agreements between the United States and Canada might provide a precedent for broader multilateral agreements.

---

imports; the gain to consumers is an important part of the overall gain from trade. Business executives and politicians, in contrast, emphasize the gain from greater access to export markets, and often look on cheap imports as a nuisance, or worse. (Viner used to observe that we do not much like foreigners to send cheap goods to us; and the cheaper they are, the less we like it.) In my opinion, it would be desirable for economists and politicians to move closer together. Economists at times place too much emphasis on the gains to consumers, and too little on the gains that exporters reap from greater access to foreign markets (Wonnacott and Wonnacott 1981). Politicians generally pay too little attention to the benefits to consumers.

Another option would be to compromise, picking an intermediate course, looking toward an agreement involving sectoral or partial tariff cuts. Such a course seems to be very much a third best. It would not only be less likely to improve the efficiency of the North American economy; it would also raise a difficult problem for both the United States and Canada, of weighing relations with its North American partner against the threat to the most-favored-nation system.

ANNEX 2A   Triangular Efficiency Effects

Figure 2.2 illustrates the effects of tariffs on economic efficiency, in a simple case where a country faces a fixed world price of, say, $60. If a tariff of $10 is imposed, the domestic price rises from $60 to $70. Domestic producers respond by increasing their output (in this example, from 800 to 1,000 units); they clearly gain from the higher price. Specifically, they have a $10 windfall on each of the 800 units they would have produced in any case, for a total of $8,000 shown by area 1. (This windfall goes into higher profits for firms, or higher incomes for employees, or higher returns to some other input.) There is also a further gain on the additional 200 units produced. For example, there is a gain on the nine-hundredth unit—its marginal cost of production is $65, but it can be sold at the $70 price, for a windfall of $5. The sum of all such gains on the units from 800 to 1,000 is equal to area 2. Thus, the total benefit that producers reap from the tariff is a combination of areas 1 + 2.

Consumers are, however, clearly worse off as a result of the tariff. They respond to the higher price by reducing their purchases (in the example, from 2,300 units to 2,000). On the 2,000 units they would purchase in any event, the burden imposed by the tariff is $20,000; that is, a $10 higher price on each of the 2,000 units, as shown by the combined areas 1 + 2 + 3 + 4. Consumers also lose on the units from 2,000 to 2,300 that they no longer buy. Consider, for example, unit number 2,200. Some buyer would have been willing to pay $63 for it (shown by the height of the demand curve at b). In the free trade case, that unit would have been available at the world price of $60; thus the loss to the consumer from not having that unit is $3. Accordingly, consumers lose area 5 on the 300 units not purchased because of the tariff and the higher price that results. The total loss to consumers from the tariff is accordingly the sum of areas 1 through 5.

FIGURE 2.2 **Triangular efficiency effects**

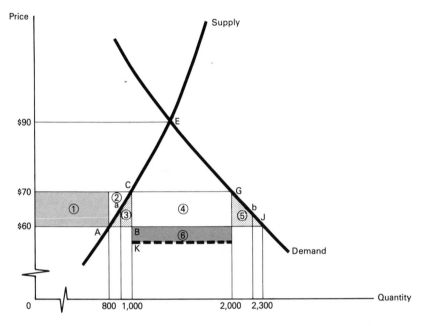

There is also one other actor, the government, which collects tariffs equal to area 4 (the $10 tariff collected on each of 1,000 units of imports). To get the net result of the tariff, we take the gains of areas 1 + 2 to producers and area 4 to the government, and subtract the losses of areas 1 through 5 to consumers—leaving a net cost of the tariffs equal to triangles 3 + 5. To estimate the costs of the home tariff, or the gains on the import side from moving to free trade, the simplest and most basic approach is to add up the triangular areas such as 1 and 5 in the various protected industries.

CHANGES IN INTERNATIONAL PRICES

However, this rather simple approach leaves out some important complications. One is the effect that a tariff can have on international prices. In figure 2.2, we have thus far assumed that the imposition of

FIGURE 2.3   **Cost to exporting country**

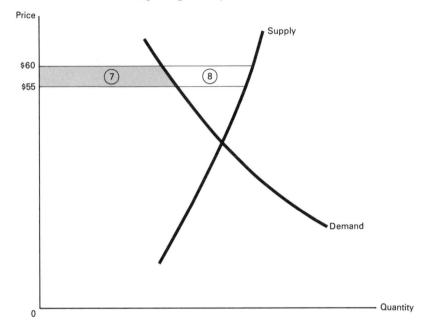

the tariff causes no change in the world price; it remains stable at $60. Thus, the domestic consumer bears the full burden of the $10 tariff when the domestic price rises to $70. But, in fact, when a tariff is imposed, the international price may fall, because the importing country is buying less on the world markets. For example, when a $15 tariff is imposed, the world price may fall by $5. This is illustrated by the dashed line at K in figure 2.2. Here, a $15 tariff (KC) results in a $5 fall in the world price (KB) and a $10 rise in the domestic price (BC).

In this case, the government's tariff falls not only on the domestic consumer (area 4, BC x CG), but also partly on the foreign producer, who receives $5 less per unit on 1,000 units (area 6). As a result, the country imposing a tariff may gain. It will do so if the amount extracted from foreign producers (area 6) exceeds the triangular efficiency losses (3 + 5).

However, the foreign country loses, as illustrated in figure 2.3. As the price of their exports is depressed by $5, their producers lose areas

7 and 8 (for exactly the same reason that the importing country's producers gained areas 1 + 2 in figure 2.2). This loss clearly exceeds the gain of foreign consumers (area 7) which comes from the lower price in the exporting country. The clear net cost (area 8) imposed on foreign countries by our tariff explains the most striking feature of international tariff negotiations—every country is eager for its trading partners to cut their tariffs.

These two diagrams also illustrate one of the major reasons why international negotiations over tariffs occur in the first place. It is hard to generate any enthusiam for cutting one's own tariffs. Even though the benefits that domestic producers reap from the tariff (1 + 2) are smaller than the cost to consumers (1 through 5), producer interest is likely to be concentrated politically, while the interests of consumers are diffuse and nebulous. Furthermore, the transfer extracted from the trading partners (6) may more than offset the triangular efficiency losses (3 + 5); there thus may be a net loss from cutting the domestic tariff. However, any reduction in tariffs that foreign nations can be persuaded to make will be a clear gain. With an exchange of tariff cuts, the transfers among trading partners (areas such as 6) may more or less balance out, leaving overall efficiency gains (such as triangles 3 and 5).

3   Why Now?

The possibility of freer trade has been a recurrent theme in the relationship between the United States and Canada. Indeed, it goes back to the 1840s, even before the provinces were unified into the Canadian Nation in 1867.

This raises the obvious question: Why now? Why have negotiations been opened between the two countries at this time? Why not in 1955, 1965 or 1975?

To answer this question, we must look at it primarily from the Canadian viewpoint—for the very simple reason that the initiative had to come from Canada. Because of the huge disparity in the sizes of the two economies, Canada is more concerned with maintaining national sovereignty and independence; the United States need give no thought to the possibility that it will be swallowed up by its smaller neighbor to the north. An initiative from the US side would have been looked on suspiciously in Canada, perhaps as a power grab threatening the very existence of the nation. If free trade negotiations are to have any chance of success, it is essential that Canadians go into them with the assurance that it is their decision, the result of a careful calculation of the national interest. This point has been well understood in the United States: any US initiative for a comprehensive bilateral trading arrangement would be the kiss of death; the first step had to come from Canada. It did so with the Prime Minister's speech to Parliament on 26 September 1985, announcing the Canadian government's desire to pursue a new trade agreement with the United States.

This chapter addresses the question of why the Canadian government came to this decision. It was the result of three interrelated factors:

• a growing realization among the business community, academics, and politicians of how difficult it is for Canadian manufacturing to achieve large-scale, efficient production without access to a large market; economies of scale mean that the gains from free trade can be large

• the changing character of the Canadian economy, and of its international trading relationships

• fear that protectionism in the United States threatens existing Canadian trade.

Thus, the Canadian initiative was inspired both by a hope for a better trading relationship, and a fear that things might get worse without major new initiatives. While fear has been important in bringing the two nations to the bargaining table, it has meant that the chances for success are perhaps not as great as they would have been in less threatening times. For example, the United States is now less willing than it would have been fifteen years ago to provide Canada the assurances that it wants on the subsidy issue. However, one cannot hope to negotiate at an ideal time, under ideal circumstances. Simon Reisman—the chief Canadian negotiator in the free trade talks—has noted the difficulty of finding a time when both countries simultaneously wanted bilateral free trade (1984, p. 43):

Canadian interest in reciprocity traditionally has peaked during periods of economic difficulty or when Canada has been frustrated by difficulties with other trading partners, particularly the United Kingdom and Western Europe. The United States, by contrast, traditionally has turned inward and reverted to more protectionist policies in the face of hard times. Thus there has been a recurrent mismatch of goals and interests in matters of trade policy.

The time will never be perfect. If the opportunity for free trade is missed now, it is unlikely to recur in the near future.

The first of the above three points provided the theme for chapter 2. In this chapter, the second and third points will be studied. (We repeat that the primary emphasis will be on Canadian viewpoints; US concerns will be treated in detail in later chapters.) This chapter will conclude with a summary of the negotiating positions of the two countries—what each hopes to get out of the current talks. This will lay the background for the final chapters, which cover some of the problems the negotiators face.

FIGURE 3.1   **Canadian exports, as percentage of GNP**

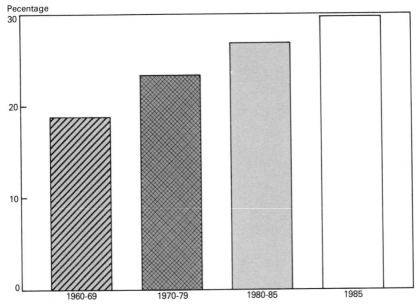

Source: Economic Council of Canada (1986, p. 84).

The Changing Pattern of Canadian Trade

Three major developments have increased the dependence of Canada on the US market, and have underlined the importance of access to the US market as a source of Canadian prosperity. In recent decades:

• Exports have risen as a percentage of GNP.

• Exports have increasingly been directed toward the United States.

• Manufactured goods are making up an increasing share of exports, with agricultural and mining products declining relatively.

Figure 3.1 shows the substantial increase in merchandise exports as a percentage of Canadian GNP. (On the other hand, exports of services were quite stable, at about 4.5 percent of GNP. An increase in

FIGURE 3.2   **Destination of Canadian merchandise exports**

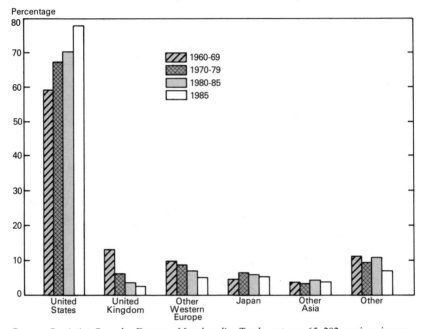

Source: Statistics Canada, Exports: Merchandise Trade, cat. no. 65–202, various issues, and Dominion Bureau of Statistics, Review of Foreign Trade, various issues.

investment income approximately offset the fall in travel receipts, as a percentage of GNP.) At the same time, the share of Canadian exports going to the United States was increasing from from 59.3 percent in the 1960s to 70.1 percent between 1980 and 1985 (figure 3.2). The Japanese share increased, as did the share of the rest of Asia. The decline in share of Canadian exports was concentrated in Western Europe, particularly the United Kingdom. This change in shares was the result of strong economic forces—the rise of the Japanese and other Asian economies, and the powerful attraction of the close US market. The development of intra-European ties, and particularly the entry of the United Kingdom into the Economic Community, contributed to the decline in the share of Canadian exports going to Western Europe. As noted in chapter 1, Canadian policy was from time to time

FIGURE 3.3   **Commodity composition of Canadian exports**

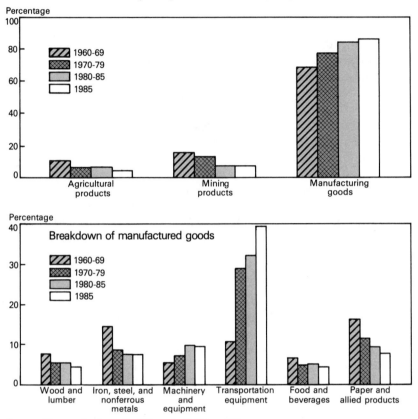

Source: Economic Council of Canada (1986, p. 84).

aimed unsuccessfully at reducing the share of exports going to the United States, and increasing Western Europe's share.

The third main development has been the increasing share of manufactured goods in Canadian merchandise exports—from 68.8 percent in the 1960s to 86.0 percent in the early 1980s (figure 3.3). One of the traditional economic fears of Canadians—that they are in danger of becoming mere "hewers of wood and drawers of water" for their cousins south of the border—should be allowed to fade into history. Of the increases in manufacturing exports, by far the largest occurred in transportation equipment; by 1985, this category accounted for 39.6 percent of total Canadian merchandise exports. This sharp increase was in large part a result of the US-Canadian Auto Pact of 1965, which provided for duty-free trade in vehicles and original equipment parts; it led to a rapid growth of two-way automotive trade. The general machinery and equipment category also accounted for an increasing share of Canadian exports, while the shares declined for agricultural products, mining products, wood and lumber, iron and steel and nonferrous metals, food and beverages, and paper and allied products.

These changes have provided both a carrot and a stick for Canadian policymakers. The rapid increase in manufactured exports to the United States have provided a carrot, in the form of a rich US market, particularly for industries (notably automobiles) that have duty-free access. However, the high level of manufactured exports also represents a stick—the threat of what might happen if access to the US market were restricted.

The Changing Nature of Protection: Canadian Concerns over "Contingent Protection"

In recent years, two interrelated developments in US commercial policy have caused concern in Canada, and have been motivating forces in the Canadian decision to propose negotiations over a possible free trade arrangement. First has been the concern that the United States was in danger of backsliding into a protectionism that would endanger Canadian exports. As the US trade deficit has ballooned in recent years, protectionist pressures have increased in the United States, and Canadians have become increasingly worried about possible future legislation.

The second Canadian worry is the change in the nature of international protection, with US protection being a matter of particular concern. As tariff rates have been negotiated downward in the Kennedy and Tokyo rounds, there has been a movement in the United States and elsewhere (including Canada) to formalize and tighten trade remedy laws and procedures which are designed to protect domestic industries from excessive or unfair foreign competition. The four major forms of US trade remedies are:[1]

- escape clause actions

- antidumping duties

- countervailing duties (CVDs) on subsidized exports

- action against other unfair foreign competition.

ESCAPE CLAUSE ACTIONS

When the US International Trade Commission (USITC), after an investigation, concludes that imports are a "substantial cause of serious injury, or the threat thereof" to a domestic industry (Trade Act of 1974, Section 201), it may recommend adjustment assistance or temporary import relief. Within 60 days of a recommendation by the USITC for import relief, the President is required to provide it unless he determines that it is not in the national economic interest. It was under this procedure that temporary duties were imposed on Canadian shakes and shingles at the time the bilateral trade negotiations were opened in 1986. (The tariff began at 35 percent and is scheduled to be phased out over five years.)

ANTIDUMPING DUTIES

Antidumping duties are provided if two conditions are met: the Department of Commerce determines that the good is sold at less than its fair value; and the USITC determines that, as a result, an industry in the United States is "materially injured, or is threatened with material injury."

---

1. For details, see US House of Representatives, Committee on Ways and Means (1984), and Hufbauer and Rosen (1986).

COUNTERVAILING DUTIES

Countervailing duties (CVDs) follow similar investigative procedures by Commerce and the USITC. In this case, the USITC again determines whether or not there is material injury, while Commerce determines if the foreign good is subsidized—a controversial and complex issue addressed in the next chapter. Of the four types of trade remedies, this is the most important source of Canadian concern.

CVD and antidumping duties are similar to one another, but different from escape clause actions, in four important respects:

• The material injury test of antidumping and countervailing duties is less difficult to meet than the escape clause test. "Material injury" is harm which is not inconsequential, immaterial, or unimportant. The "substantial cause of serious injury" in the escape clause means "a cause which is important and not less than any other cause."

• CVD and antidumping duties are aimed at unfair foreign practices (subsidies and dumping), whereas escape clause actions do not imply foreign misbehavior.

• Escape clause actions are intended to be temporary, to ease the adjustment process, whereas CVD and antidumping duties are intended to last as long as the subsidies or dumping continue.

• The President has discretion on whether to use escape clause remedies, but positive findings by the USITC and Commerce in the CVD and antidumping cases require the automatic application of tariffs.

UNFAIR PRACTICES

Under Section 301 of the Trade Act of 1974, the President is empowered to suspend concessions to foreign nations or impose import restrictions if a foreign nation denies the United States benefits under any trade agreement, or unreasonably restricts US commerce. Section 337 of the Tariff Act of 1930 requires the USITC to investigate unfair trade methods; in practice, the majority of cases have involved patent or trademark infringement. Subject to the President's disapproval, the USITC may issue cease and desist orders.

These trade remedy laws—and particularly the countervailing duty law—are seen as problems in Canada, because they make access to the US market *unpredictable,* and because Canadian exporters can become bogged down in *expensive and time-consuming procedures.* Rodney Grey, who acted as many years as a Canadian trade negotiator, has been particularly outspoken on such measures, which he labels "contingent protection." Such *flexible* arrangements have increased in importance as tariffs have been reduced. Grey criticizes contingent protection on the ground that it:

Requires a large bureaucratic establishment, which must be presumed to be capable of having available a detailed knowledge of a large number of transactions at any given time. . . . This means, in effect, that only a large industrial state can effectively work a contingency system. . . . In this important sense, the contingency system is biased in favor of the large industrial countries.

In a second sense, the contingency system is power-oriented. Industries in small countries, if they are to compete on world markets, must produce in plants of optimum size, . . . [exporting] perhaps three quarters of the output of their plants. An antidumping or a countervailing duty action against exports of an optimum-sized plant in a small country can be particularly damaging, simply because it affects such a large portion of the plant's output. . . .

. . . Examination of the contingency system in practice will show that the search for a system of rules designed as a partial substitute for the crude interplay of power relationships has resulted in little more than what could be called "power-oriented" rules.

It is not at all clear that the developing system of contingent protection . . . will be *as a system* less restrictive or less interventionist, less trade distorting, less trade diverting, less costly, than the older system—which relied in the main on published schedules of import fees. . . .[2]

---

2. Grey (1983a, pp. 248–50); italics in original. See also Grey (1982) and Grey (1984).

Grey's first argument, that small countries are at a disadvantage because of the bureaucracies required to enforce contingent protection, is not very convincing. Small countries have been quite capable of enforcing extensive and complex protection.

However, the United States does have one additional advantage as the largest participant in the world economy. In the establishment of the General Agreement on Tariffs and Trade (GATT), the rules often followed US practices closely; to a significant extent, the GATT articles codify US views. While this in a sense gives an advantage to the United States, it may also be desirable from a small-country viewpoint. Because protectionist actions by large countries can cause such major damage to other countries, with relatively limited domestic damage, it is in the interests of the smaller countries to have a set of rules by which the largest country is most likely to live.

In one sense, the dangers that "contingent protection" pose for Canada are perhaps even worse than suggested by Grey. After all, Canada is at least a medium-sized country, not a small one, and on that account should be in a relatively good position. But the problem is not just the size of the country, or the percentage of exports from vulnerable plants. In addition, the problem is how heavily the exports are focused on a single country, where the application of import restraints will fall in a single blow on the exporting firm. A small country with its exports spread among a dozen major countries may be much less vulnerable than Canada, with its very heavy dependence on a single foreign market, the United States. Canada's problem is that it has its eggs so concentrated in a single basket. It is not surprising that concerns regarding US "contingent protection" are voiced so strongly in Canada.

At the same time, we should not exaggerate the disadvantages of "contingent protection" compared to the old system with higher tariffs. It is not just the contingent protection system that works to the disadvantage of the smaller countries; it is *any* system of protection. The smaller countries have the biggest stake in an open international trading system. It is not clear whether smaller countries are better off with moderate but stable tariffs, or low tariffs supplemented with contingent barriers. The former permanently reduce opportunities in foreign markets. The latter allow firms into the foreign markets—but only on an uncertain and risky basis. That, in a sense, is the problem of Canadian industry: with US tariffs low and falling, Canadian producers are enticed by the closeness of the US market. But it is a market that cannot altogether be counted upon.

Despite the attention paid to US countervailing duties, the risks to Canada should not be exaggerated. It is true that the United States has taken several CVD actions against Canadian exports in the past year (pork, fish), and a preliminary decision was made against the important Canadian lumber industry (whose annual exports to the United States have been running at about $3 billion). However, such actions have not been common. A recent study by the staff of the International Monetary Fund (Anjaria, Kirmani, and Petersen 1985, p. 110) summarizes CVD actions over the period from mid-1982 to the end of 1984. Of the 37 actions taken by the United States during that period, none was directed at Canadian exports. (In the same period,

Canada took only 2 actions, neither directed at US exports.) If Canadian firms sometimes feel that they are playing Russian roulette in their trade with the United States, they can perhaps take some solace in the fact that there are many chambers, only one of which is loaded.

Nevertheless, it is not only CVD actions, but the *threat* thereof, which cause concern in Canada, where "the very existence of a mandatory, legalistic, quasi-judicial process of investigating imports" is seen as "a significant deterrent to trade because of its potential use as a form of harassment."[3] Thus, for example, the CVD investigation into Canadian lumber imports, undertaken in 1986, was interpreted as harassment because a similar investigation several years ago had ended with the determination that there were no countervailable subsidies.

Negotiating Objectives

Both nations have talked in terms of reducing tariffs and freeing trade. But their detailed statement of objectives shows considerable difference in coverage and emphasis. Canada's broad negotiating objectives were set out in a report by James F. Kelleher, Minister for International Trade (1985). They include the desire to:[4]

- *save jobs* in the short run, and *create jobs* in the longer term

- strengthen the economic basis for *cultural objectives*

- *secure and enhance access* to the US market by *enshrining* a better set of rules for trade

- develop a *more predictable* environment for trade and investment.

Mr. Kelleher followed these items with a reiteration of Canada's commitment to the multilateral system of the GATT, which "should remain the cornerstone of our international trade policy." This might be listed as an additional objective: to keep any agreement *within GATT articles,* or keep any need for waivers sufficiently limited as not to create a significant threat to the GATT system.

---

3. Carmichael, Edward A. (1985, p. 31).
4. Throughout the summaries of the Canadian and US positions, all italics have been added.

Mr. Kelleher also listed a number of US trade barriers that many Canadian producers thought could and should be reduced:

• the manner in which access to the US market can be frustrated by the use of *trade remedy laws*

• the ease with which imports from Canada are swept up in *measures aimed at others*

• the continual threat of *unilateral changes* in the rules of the game

• *Buy America* provisions at the federal and state levels

• *tariffs*.

Finally, Mr. Kelleher listed the *inadequacy of mechanisms to resolve disputes*.

US objectives were laid out by Trade Representative Clayton K. Yeutter in his report to the President (1985). In informal discussions, representatives of the private sector and members of Congress had emphasized two major objectives, namely to:

• reduce Canadian barriers to international commerce, including *tariffs* and *nontariff barriers*, obstacles to US *investment*, and regulations that impede US exports of *services*

• limit the use of *subsidies*. A great many US industries are concerned over Canadian governmental assistance programs, at both the federal and provincial levels, which allegedly result in subsidized competition.

Both Kelleher and Yeutter also reported progress on eight items listed at the Shamrock summit; these topics have been folded into the broader negotiations on freer trade:

• national treatment with respect to *government procurement*

• simplification of *regulations* that impeded trade

• improvement in the *Air Transport Agreement*

• maintaining and extending open access to each other's *energy* markets, including oil, natural gas, electricity, and coal

• reduction in *trade barriers*

• facilitation of *travel* for business purposes

• reduction in tariffs and nontariff barriers to trade in *high-technology* goods and services

• cooperation to protect *intellectual property rights*, including trade in counterfeit goods and other abuses of copyright and patent law.

Although there is substantial overlap in the interests of the two countries—as illustrated by their agreement to discuss the eight early topics—there are also major differences in emphasis. The stated US objectives are to reduce existing barriers to trade in goods, services, and capital flows, and deal with the subsidy problem. While Canada would, of course, welcome a reduction in existing US trade barriers, such barriers are not at the top of the list of Canadian concerns. Rather, the Canadian statement concentrates on the *risk of nasty surprises*—that is, the risk that Canada will be harmed when competing US producers ask for relief under US trade remedy laws, or sideswiped by the application of measures aimed at others. (An example often cited in Canada was the US import surcharge of 1971, aimed at encouraging other nations to realign their exchange rates. The surcharge applied to dutiable imports from Canada, even though Canada had a flexible exchange rate and its dollar had already strengthened in terms of the US currency.)

Indeed, concern that access to US markets be *assured* is by far the strongest single message in Canadian statements regarding trade negotiations. It not only runs through the Kelleher Report; it has been repeatedly emphasized by Pat Carney, Kelleher's replacement as Minister for International Trade. It also was a central theme of Prime Minister Brian Mulroney in his statement to the House of Commons (26 September, 1985) announcing the government's intention to pursue bilateral trade talks with the United States. Mr. Mulroney spoke of the need for a "more predictable" trading relationship with the United States, which might be achieved through a "legally binding" agreement. In a four-page statement, the need to "secure" access to the US market was mentioned no fewer than four times.

This difference in emphasis between the United States and Canada is perhaps surprising, because "contingent protection"—with all its uncertainties—has become more significant in both countries as tariff barriers have fallen. Antidumping duties are an important part of Canadian trade legislation, and Canada as well as the United States has developed quasi-judicial procedures for hearing trade disputes. Indeed, it is sometimes the same industry that feels the impact of contingent protection on both sides of the border. For example, in early 1985, the Canadian Import Tribunal imposed dumping duties on imports of steel well-drilling products from four countries, including the United States. A year later, the US government imposed penalty duties on similar products from Canada, following a finding by the Commerce Department that Canadian exports had been subsidized and sold at less than fair market value in Canada.

The reason Canada places so much more emphasis on predictability and security of access is, however, quite straightforward. Because Canada is so heavily dependent on the US market, it is particularly vulnerable to the unexpected imposition of trade barriers by the United States.

One of the greatest concerns of both governments is the subsidy issue. Although subsidies are far from the most important deterrent to efficient trade between the United States and Canada, they represent one of the most difficult political issues in the current negotiations; they are perhaps the most likely problem on which negotiations may fail. Subsidies were mentioned as one of the two major issues by Yeutter, and the possibility of US countervailing duties in response to real or perceived subsidies is one of the nasty surprises that most worries the Canadian government. They will provide the focus of chapter 4.

4   Trade Remedy Laws

Although empirical studies suggest that substantial efficiency gains could be made through a bilateral free trade arrangement, negotiations will not be smooth and easy; there are many topics of potential conflict. The next two chapters will look at some of the major areas of disagreement.

This chapter will pick up where the previous one ended, with subsidies. Both countries have strong views on this subject. In the United States, there is concern that subsidies, industrial policies, and gimmicks of the Canadian government will put some US producers at a disadvantage. In Canada, US countervailing duty (CVD) procedures are feared as the unpredictable wild card in the free trade deck. As a background for the subsidy issue, the early pages of this chapter will review the US-Canadian Automotive Agreement of 1965 (the "Auto Pact"), which was aimed, among other things, at defusing a potential conflict over subsidies. This will be followed by a discussion of the general economic issues raised by subsidies, and by a review of questions raised by the recent US CVD case in softwood lumber. Finally, we will consider a matter of particular concern to Canadians: their fear that US CVD law will interfere with Canadian social policies, such as unemployment insurance and regional development programs.

The study of specific cases will mean that a disproportionate amount of time is spent on the subsidy question—which is, after all, only one of a dozen or so major negotiating issues. However, there is an advantage in going into a single problem in detail, to get some idea of the complexity and subtlety of the issues facing the two countries in their current negotiations.

The focus of this chapter will be on Canadian subsidies, alleged and actual; US subsidies are practically ignored. This is not because of an absence of US subsidies; an extensive list could easily be compiled. Agriculture is the biggest problem, where an export subsidy war between the United States and the European Community (EC) threatens to severely disrupt the overseas markets of Canada, Australia, and other exporters. Even though some issues raised by US agricultural subsidies may be addressed in a bilateral framework—most notably, the Canadian countervailing action against US corn—progress toward a satisfactory overall solution obviously requires a broader forum, and, in particular, one that includes the EC. Outside agriculture, US subsidies are not central concerns in Canada, except, perhaps, as a way of rebutting US complaints regarding Canadian subsidies. Therefore, the focus of this chapter will be one-sidedly on Canadian subsidies and US responses, because that is the side on which the major bilateral problems lie.

Background to the Subsidy Issue: The Automotive Agreement of 1965

Although the subsidy issue poses one of the major dangers to US-Canadian relations, it paradoxically provided the initial impetus to the Auto Pact, which represented an early step toward duty-free trade between the two countries. Although the Auto Pact prevented a major confrontation over subsidies in the 1960s, the problem of automotive subsidies has continued to lurk in the background. Recently, it has begun to attract attention again as a result of complaints in Michigan over Canada's system of remission of duties on automotive imports from overseas.

PRELUDE TO THE AUTO PACT: THE CANADIAN SEARCH FOR LONGER PRODUCTION RUNS

In the late 1950s, Canadians became increasingly concerned over the unhealthy condition of the automobile industry. In spite of wages about 30 percent less than in the United States, the Canadian industry was a high-cost producer, protected by a 17.5 percent tariff on cars and a Canadian content requirement. Provided that their cars contained domestic content equal to at least 60 percent of their total value, automobile producers in Canada were permitted duty-free importation of parts equal to the remaining 40 percent.[1]

The Bladen Report

To investigate the causes of inefficiency, the Canadian government appointed Dean Vincent Bladen of the University of Toronto as a one-man Royal Commission. Bladen put his finger on short, fragmented production runs as the cause of the Canadian industry's problems. The Canadian producers of automobiles—which were subsidiaries of GM, Ford, and other US firms—were producing almost as wide a range of models in Canada as in the United States, but only a small volume of each. As a solution, Bladen suggested the idea of *extended content*. To qualify for duty-free importation of parts, automobile companies operating in Canada would still have to meet the requirement that Canadian parts and other Canadian content equal at least 60 percent of their Canadian automobile sales. However—and this was Bladen's principal innovation—the Canadian-produced "content" would not have to be actually "contained" in cars sold in Canada. It could be exported instead. Indeed, as long as the 60 percent production target were met, automotive companies would qualify for duty-free importation of any amount of completed automobiles and parts. To meet their production target, additional imports would of course require additional exports.

This in fact was the purpose of Bladen's proposal—to allow auto producers in Canada to specialize, exporting much of their output in exchange for additional imports, provided only that they meet their overall production targets. By specializing in relatively few parts and models, producers would be able to achieve longer, more efficient production runs.[2]

---

1. Engines were excluded from the duty-free provisions; they were subject to a 25 percent duty. For the fine points of Canadian automotive protection in the early 1960s, see the Royal Commission on the Automobile Industry, *Report* (1962), or Beigie (1970).
2. For details on how the Bladen proposals would have contributed to efficiency, see Wonnacott (1965). A much more critical view may be found in Johnson (1963).

The Duty Remission Schemes of 1962 and 1963

While the Bladen proposals provided the starting point for the Canadian policy review, the policies that actually emerged were quite different. In their new policies of 1962 and 1963, the Canadian government added two important twists that caused problems south of the border. First, the statutory 25 percent duty on automatic transmissions, which had previously been suspended, was reinstated. Second, for each additional $1 in exports of automobiles or parts over and above the exports of the 1961–62 base period, auto producers in Canada would earn duty remission on $1 of imports of automatic transmissions or engines. They would still have to meet the domestic content requirement: each Canadian car would have to include 60 percent in Canadian value added. (As before—and in contrast to the extended content idea of Bladen—Canadian content would have to actually be contained in cars sold in Canada.)

The implications of this policy were quite different from those of the Bladen Plan. Whereas the Bladen Plan would have permitted additional imports for additional exports on a one-to-one basis, the new policies of the Canadian government required a *two*-for-one response. For example, to earn duty-free importation of engines, a Canadian automobile producer would have to do two things:

• increase exports by an amount equal to the value of the engines being imported

• increase the input of other Canadian parts to compensate for the engines, and thus maintain a 60 percent Canadian content.

The objectives of the 1962–63 policies were not only to increase the length of production runs by encouraging exports, but also to increase the overall quantity of automotive production in Canada. That is, the Canadian government wanted not only to increase the efficiency of the automotive industry, but also to decrease the trade deficit in automobiles, which had contributed to the overall trade deficit that had caused so much concern during the preceding decade.

Because auto makers who increased their exports could thereby obtain the rebate of the 25 percent tariff on engines or automatic transmissions, the question arose as to whether Canada was providing a 25 percent subsidy to exports. A number of US parts producers thought so, and complained to the government. When they failed to receive an adequate response, a Wisconsin radiator producer filed suit to force the government to impose a countervailing duty. Most observers believed that the plaintiff would win. Faced with the prospect of a US countervailing duty and Canadian retaliation, the two governments initiated hurried negotiations that ended in the Auto Pact of 1965. Although some officials in the US and Canadian governments thought that the pact might lead to a broader agreement, a grand free trade design was not the primary motive. Rather, the pact was much more mundane; it was primarily a damage-control operation, aimed at preventing a major trade confrontation.

THE AUTOMOTIVE AGREEMENT OF 1965: DUTY-FREE TRADE IN VEHICLES AND ORIGINAL EQUIPMENT PARTS

The Auto Pact provided for duty-free passage of new automobiles and original equipment parts, subject to certain conditions. Specifically, the privilege of duty-free imports into Canada was confined to automobile manufacturers who were required to

• maintain the preagreement ratio of Canadian production of cars to their Canadian sales of cars (and, in any case, not less than 75 percent)

• maintain, in the production of vehicles in Canada, a level of Canadian value added, measured in dollar terms, equal to that in the 1964 model year.

The first of these conditions meant that automobile companies in Canada were committed to assemble almost as many cars as they sold there; under the pact, Canada could be a net exporter of *completed cars* to the United States, but not a significant net importer.

In addition, there were discussions between the Canadian government and Canadian automobile producers, to which the US government was not a party, which resulted in the producers' writing "letters of undertaking," committing themselves to increase Canadian *value added* by at least 60 percent of the growth in their Canadian sales, plus an additional C$260 million by the 1968 model year (approximately US$240 million at the exchange rate of the time).

Observe that the safeguards reflected a Canadian preference for automobile assembly over parts. Because of the first condition associated with the pact, Canada could not run a significant deficit in assembled automobiles with the United States. But it could run a significant deficit in parts. In fact, the overall bilateral balance in automotive trade has fluctuated widely, from a Canadian deficit of C$600 million in 1966 to a surplus of C$200 million in 1971 to a deficit of C$1,400 million in 1975 to a surplus of C$5,100 million in 1985 (as measured in Canadian statistics).[3]

From the Canadian viewpoint, the automotive agreement provided everything the Bladen Plan would have achieved, and then some. Canadian value added was maintained at the preceding ratios, plus the C$260 million. Furthermore, the rationalization of the Canadian industry was made much easier and less expensive by the elimination of US duties ranging from 6.5 percent to 8.5 percent. The growth of two-way trade could now take place without overcoming a tariff barrier; Canadian producers did not have to absorb US duties when exporting to the United States. Canadian production could be concentrated in the automotive products in which Canada was comparatively most efficient (subject to the assembly requirement).

From the US viewpoint, the agreement prevented a potentially nasty confrontation with Canada, in which the Canadian subsidiaries of US auto firms might have been caught in the middle. For example, they would have been the first losers if Canada had responded to a US countervailing duty by raising the domestic content requirement to 70 percent or 80 percent. The agreement permitted the United States to compete for as much as 40 percent of the increase in the Canadian market (less the US$240 million).

The letters of understanding were, however, a continuous source of friction. During the ratification proceedings, a number of senators objected that the Canadian government had gone outside the government-to-government negotiations, to impose unilaterally a market-sharing agreement on the automobile companies. The US government understood these letters, and the other two "safeguards" in the agreement itself, to be transitional measures, aimed at the short-run

---

3. The US Department of Commerce measured the bilateral US deficit in automotive trade with Canada at US$5.7 billion (or C$7.8 billion) in 1985.

period when the Canadian industry was being exposed to US competition and was rationalizing. However, the Canadian government made them a permanent fixture of their automotive policy, refusing to reconsider them during the "comprehensive" 1968 review called for in the agreement—even though the bilateral automotive trade balance had by that time swung over $700 million, leaving Canada with a small surplus.[4] Philip Trezise, who had helped negotiate the agreement as an official of the State Department, reports (1985, pp. 67–68) that, "Within the US executive branch, and among some members of Congress as well, the view hardened that the Canadians not only had rigged the agreement in the first place but were now acting in bad faith by refusing to modify in any way the terms which had 'unfairly' converted the American trade surplus into a deficit." So strong were the feelings against the agreement that, at the time of the historic Camp David meeting in August 1971, a tentative decision was taken to announce an abrogation of the Auto Pact. The intent was not to actually terminate the agreement, but to press Canada into bending on the safeguards. A Treasury press release including an abrogation announcement—together with the decisions to impose price and wage controls, suspend gold convertibility, and impose an import surcharge— had already been run off before objections from the State Department caused its reconsideration and a deletion of the passage on the Auto Pact.

Resentment over the Canadian safeguards was slow to disappear. In 1975, the Senate Finance Committee asked the US International Trade Commission (USITC) to investigate whether Canada had fully complied with the letter and spirit of the agreement by phasing out the so-called "transitional provisions." The USITC concluded (1976, p. v) that Canada had not done so. Nevertheless, opposition to the agreement gradually dissipated in the United States, even as the bilateral US deficit in automotive trade with Canada widened to almost $6 billion by 1985. Perhaps the widening deficit was itself a reason why frictions over the safeguards dwindled. Canadian production surpassed the safeguards by such a wide margin—perhaps because of the decline in the exchange value of the Canadian dollar—that the

---

4. For a chronology of the major developments in US-Canadian automotive trade, see Moroz (1985, table 1).

safeguards became less important. When rumblings were heard from Michigan in 1986, it was not over safeguards and the encouragement of production by US automobile subsidiaries in Canada, but rather over the way in which Canada was using the Auto Pact and duty-free access to the US market to attract Japanese investment.

Although the Auto Pact was successful in two main objectives— avoiding a confrontation and permitting longer, more efficient production runs in the Canadian auto industry—it does not in itself provide much ground for optimism that the current negotiations will be smooth or easy. On the contrary, it highlights just how different are perceptions on the two sides of the border—in spite of the common language, similar culture, and widespread view in each country (particularly Canada) that they understand the other rather well. In Canada, the intense feeling of vulnerability leads to the view that Canadian industry must be provided with safeguards—or, in plain language, with nontariff protection. Indeed, in his detailed study of the Auto Pact, Carl Beigie (1970, p. 48) concluded that political pressures were so strong that the Canadian government would not have signed the agreement without the letters of undertaking from the auto producers. More recently (1986), Robert White, President of the Canadian Automobile Workers, has argued for continued Canadian protection from US automotive competition.

In the United States, there is a strong feeling that fairness requires symmetry or reciprocity. It is unlikely that Congress would agree to a broad free trade agreement similar to the Auto Pact, with safeguards solely on the Canadian side, or with any other major asymmetric provision that clearly favors Canada. Furthermore, the letters of understanding that accompanied the Auto Pact have caused concern in the United States that the Canadian government may enter agreements with Canadian companies (particularly the subsidiaries of foreign firms) that substantially modify and undercut potential US gains from a government-to-government treaty.

Finally, if a broad agreement on free trade proves impossible, it is hard to see the Auto Pact as a blueprint for a fallback position involving sectoral agreements in other industries. The Auto Pact was a result of too many special features of that time and that industry—including a single labor union and the domination of the Canadian industry by US subsidiaries, whose parents provided a strong political impetus for acceptance of the pact in the United States.

THE CANADIAN-JAPANESE CONNECTION:
AUTOMOTIVE SUBSIDIES ONCE MORE

The Canadian government is encouraging Japanese automobile man-ufacturers to establish plants in Canada. This is not surprising, and in and of itself can scarcely be the basis for objection by the United States. After all, the United States has already encouraged the Japanese to invest here.

However, the levers Canada is using to encourage Japanese invest-ment have led to objections. The levers include a "stick"—namely, the threat to close the Canadian market to Japanese companies that do not invest in Canada. One way to do this would be to require *all* auto firms selling in Canada to meet the Canadian production require-ments set out in the Auto Pact.[5] The levers also include three "carrots," namely:

• regional development and other grants to firms setting up manufac-turing facilities in Canada

• the provision that, by exporting Canadian-made automotive parts to the United States or elsewhere, Japanese companies can earn remission of Canadian duties on auto imports from Japan

• the prospect of duty-free entry into the US market under the Auto Pact.

The first of these levers—the exclusion of nonparticipating manu-facturers—would appear to be in violation of GATT Article XI (General Elimination of Quantitative Restrictions); at least it would be if the threat of closing the Canadian market were actually carried out. However, the clearest potential complainant on this point would be the Japanese. It is the "carrots" that have raised objections in the United States.

Particularly sensitive questions are raised by the second "carrot," because of its similarity to the duty-rebate schemes of 1962 and 1963 that precipitated the countervailing duty lawsuit that led to the Auto

---

5. From the beginning of the Auto Pact, Canada held out the option of duty-free access in auto products to other countries, *if* they met the safeguard provisions. Because of the protection afforded by the safeguards, Canada was able to do so without threatening the domestic industry. More recently, however, there has been discussion of going one step further, and *requiring* any firm selling in Canada to meet the standards of the pact.

Pact. One major purpose of the United States in entering the Auto Pact was to eliminate Canadian subsidies to automotive exports to the United States. As part of the pact, the United States removed its duties on Canadian cars and original equipment parts; in exchange, Canada permitted conditional duty-free entry and discarded the subsidy schemes of 1962 and 1963. By now using somewhat similar subsidies on exports to the United States, Canada may be running the risk of reviving the old charge of bad faith. The risk is heightened, first, because the Canadian government is reverting to a particular duty remission scheme to which the United States has already objected in the recent past; and, second, because the current Canadian duty-remission program permits Japanese firms operating in Canada to use *exports to the United States* (which are duty free under the Auto Pact) as a way to earn the rebate of Canadian duties on *imports from Japan.* As Canada is thus using the duty-free access to the US market provided by the Auto Pact as a way of reducing barriers to imports from Japan, this arrangement is much more likely to raise political heat south of the border than the old 1962–63 scheme, in which the duties at least were being rebated on *imports from the United States.* (That is, in the early 1960s, the subsidy to exports occurred when firms earned the remission of duties paid on Canadian *imports from the United States.*) Note that this duty remission provision is *quite different* from the general drawback provision used by many countries, which allows the refunding of a duty already paid on a product when *that* product is *reexported.* In the Canadian provisions, a firm can earn remission of duties on completed automobiles by exporting quite different items, such as shock absorbers, brake parts, etc. made in Canada. Unlike a duty drawback—which is recognized as legitimate under the GATT Subsidies Code—the Canadian duty rebate may reasonably be considered an export subsidy, and as such is forbidden. (Currently, the size of the subsidy is in the range of 6 percent to 9 percent.)

On the first point, the United States objected to a closely similar rebate arrangement for Volkswagen of Canada, introduced in 1978.[6]

---

6. Volkswagen Remission Order, PC 1978–2658, reproduced, in part, in annex 4A. Note particularly the phrase "exported to any country" in paragraph 2. For a discussion of some of the issues raised by the Volkswagen rebates, see Hufbauer and Shelton Erb (1984), p. 67. There are a number of recent remission orders, covering both European and Japanese companies—for example, Jaguar (PC 1985–811, 14 March 1985), and Mazda (PC 1985–812, 14 March 1985). We focus here on Honda, one important example of the rebate scheme.

Apparently as a result of US objections, and in recognition of the tariff-free entry into the US market under the Auto Pact, the Canadian government *excluded* exports to the United States when it entered a duty-remission agreement with Honda in 1980, with credit being given only for exports *to other countries* (PC 1980–2066, paragraph 2, reproduced in Annex 4A). By 1985, however, when it was revising the agreement with Honda, the Canadian government dropped the US exclusion (PC 1985–810, 14 March, paragraph 2, reaffirmed in PC 1986–637, paragraph 2, both reproduced in annex 4A). As in the 1978 VW case, rebates can once more be earned by exports *to any country,* including the United States.

The Canadian government has repeatedly expressed concern about the uncertainties and unpredictabilities of the United States on the subsidy issue. But the rebates suggest that the subsidy problem is more complex than this. While the Canadian government may well be puzzled by uncertainties over the application of the US subsidy law (for example, in the lumber case considered later in this chapter), it should have had no doubt that the United States would object to the rebate scheme; the United States has repeatedly done so in the past. The rebate scheme represents a fundamental difference of views: Canada apparently believes that such rebates are acceptable elements of commercial policy, while the United States does not.

There is some danger that the Canadian government may overplay its hand. In the normal course of events, the lion's share of the gain from the Auto Pact goes to Canada; it was the Canadian industry that was in need of rationalization through longer production runs. If Canada tries to squeeze the last ounce of gain out of the pact, there is a risk that the question will be asked in the United States, "What's in it for us?" The Canadian government fears unpleasant surprises, and rightly so. However, with the duty remission scheme, the Canadian government seems to be increasing the chance of a nasty surprise. Particularly puzzling were the March 1985 orders-in-council, which once more broadened the duty remissions to include exports to the United States.

In the summer of 1986, the United States renewed its objection to Canadian automotive rebates, in part in response to communications from Governor James Blanchard and Representative John D. Dingell (D-Mich.). As the Canadian government has already made commitments to Honda and other overseas auto firms, it may have difficulty getting out of this box. But the problem is unlikely to go away. In the past, the US automobile companies have had an interest in maintaining the Auto Pact, and have tended to insulate the pact from criticism in the United States. But, in the next few years, a new situation will arise, with East Asian firms becoming significant participants in US and Canadian production. According to current projections, production in Canada by Japanese and Korean firms may be as much as 600,000 cars by 1990 (including Suzuki's joint venture with GM). In the United States, the corresponding figure is about 1,700,000 (again including GM's joint venture, in this case with Toyota). Canada will be producing a disproportionate share of the total, and apparently is counting on becoming a significant net exporter of East Asian cars to the United States. But there is no major interest group within the United States to prevent a backlash against the import of such cars from Canada. Although the amounts of rebates are not large at present, they are growing rapidly, and they can be expected to rise sharply in the future as the production of Japanese firms in Canada increases. Furthermore, because of the history of the Auto Pact, the rebates have a symbolic significance which perhaps exceeds their importance in dollars.

Even under ideal circumstances, the rebate scheme would create strains on the Auto Pact. But the circumstances are far from ideal; Canada is adding rapidly to its capacity when the North American industry is already threatened with large excess capacity. Unless the Canadian government withdraws the rebates and undertakes not to reintroduce them, it is not clear that the strains can be contained. The duty rebate scheme represents a ticking time bomb, which threatens to explode several years down the road. If something is not done in the near future, the outcome may become very messy once factories have been built in Canada, on the assumption of a continuing rebate.

The rebate problem would exist regardless of the current free trade talks; it is unfinished business from the past, not new business. The Canadian Auto Workers union wants to keep the Auto Pact off the table in the current broad talks on free trade. But whether the subsidy issue is addressed within the broad talks or elsewhere is a secondary matter; it must be addressed somewhere. It goes without saying that the way in which the rebate issue is handled will influence the prospects for progress in the broader talks.

Subsidies: The Issue of a "Level Playing Field"

Subsidies, and the appropriate response to them, are not only one of the greatest potential difficulties for the United States and Canada in their bilateral negotiations. They also present, in the words of Gary Hufbauer and Joanna Shelton Erb, "one of the most difficult and complex sets of problems facing the world trading system."[7] Fortunately, the most intractable problem—the widespread subsidization of agricultural exports—does not come up in an acute way in bilateral negotiations. In a number of agricultural products—most notably, wheat—the United States and Canada are competitors on the world market. They have a common interest in trying to figure out ways of dealing with the trading fallout from the common agricultural policy (CAP) of the European Community, without getting involved in a full-scale subsidy war with the EC.

Three topics relating to subsidies are particularly relevant to the current bilateral negotiations—namely, the economic problems that they raise, the tangled question of how subsidies are to be defined or identified, and the response of one country to the subsidies of the other.

ECONOMIC ISSUES

Like tariffs, export subsidies can distort market forces, and can lead to trading patterns that do not correspond to comparative advantage. But, unlike tariffs, export subsidies do not necessarily harm other countries. Most obviously, the importing nation gains if there are no domestic producers (actual or potential) of the imported good—there are no competitors to be harmed, while buyers benefit from the lower price of imports. In this case, countries have no reason to impose countervailing duties. Complaints are likely to come only from other exporting nations that compete with the subsidized products on world markets—for example, complaints by Canada, Australia, and other competitors over the subsidized agricultural exports of the European Community and the United States.

---

7. Hufbauer and Shelton Erb (1984, p. xi).

FIGURE 4.1   **The effect of a subsidy**

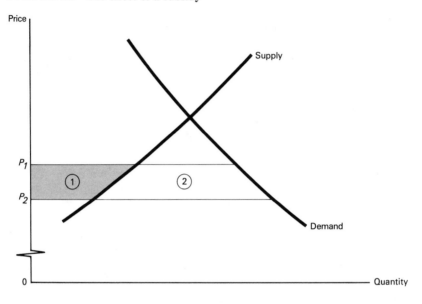

Even if there are domestic competitors who are injured by subsidized imports, the importing nation as a whole may benefit. This is illustrated in figure 4.1, which is similar to the diagrams in annex 2A. The foreign subsidization makes the price of the imported good fall from P_1 to P_2, inflicting a loss of area 1 on domestic producers. But domestic purchasers gain even more—areas 1 + 2.

It is not obvious why countries should object to foreign subsidies, at least to long-run, *consistent* subsidies to which *adjustments* may be made. A country benefits by being able to sell its exports on world markets at prices higher than they would command at home, and using the proceeds to buy imports at prices lower than they could be produced at home. The higher the foreign demand for our products, and the higher the price they fetch on world markets, the better off we are as a nation (although domestic consumers of those particular products are worse off). The cheaper the price at which we can buy imports, the better off we are as a nation (although domestic producers of those particular products are worse off). We have the same potential for gain, whether countries are willing to sell us steel cheaply because they have a comparative advantage (for example, rich sources of iron ore and coal), or because they subsidize their exports of steel—*provided* that they do so consistently, and do not simply use subsidies *as a way of unloading short-run excess production during recessions.*

Such short-run subsidies, like predatory, short-run dumping, can be harmful to the importing nation; short-run costs of adjustment and unemployment do not show up fully in figures such as 4.1. A country may use short-run export subsidies as a way of unloading adjustment costs and unemployment on its trading partners, causing a net burden on the importing country.

In sum, it is not clear that we are harmed by *long-run, consistent* export subsidies by foreign nations. Those nations may be foolish to provide such subsidies; they may be using public funds to stimulate production in uneconomic industries. But presumably the foreign nations are the ones that suffer from the distortions to international trade; it is their treasuries that have to put up the money. Why shouldn't we take advantage of cheap imports? In this regard, foreign subsidies to their exports are very different from their import duties on the goods we sell to them. Their duties unambiguously harm us—our producers generally bear some of the duty imposed by the foreign nation. With their duties, they are taxing us as well as their purchasers of imports. But subsidies are quite different: the subsidy may not only help their producers; it may also provide lower prices to our consumers. The foreign treasury may be subsidizing not only foreign producers, but also our consumers.

Finally, there is an argument, frequently made by economists, that it might be desirable to replace tariffs with subsidies to specific domestic industries, if we want to help those industries. One reason is that a subsidy is more transparent; it makes the costs of supporting an industry clearer to the public and Congress. When it comes time to pay the bills for the subsidies, Congress will have to address the costs explicitly. (In contrast, tariffs raise revenues.)

To this quasi-political argument, efficiency gains might be added. If, for example, a country were determined to aim for production of *x*-thousand units in a certain industry or group of industries, this might require quite a high tariff. The per unit subsidy required to meet the target might be substantially lower, particularly if the subsidy leads to exports. In other words, the excess costs (that is, the costs above world levels) of supporting a given quantity of output would be less with subsidies than tariffs. The desire to keep down the per unit costs of supporting the automotive industry was one of the reasons why Canada adopted the automotive programs of 1962 and 1963, with their indirect subsidies to exports.

COUNTERVAILING DUTIES

The economic issues outlined above have not, however, been central to lawmaking within the United States and Canada, or in international agreements. Even though tariffs are more clearly harmful to foreign trading partners than are export subsidies, export subsidies are flatly prohibited (except on primary products) in the GATT Code on Subsidies and Countervailing Duties, while tariffs are not prohibited by the General Agreement on Tariffs and Trade. In the International Monetary Fund (IMF), imposition of an across-the-board import surcharge (like that of the United States in 1971 or Canada in 1962) is recognized as legitimate in the face of a balance-of-payments crisis, but an across-the-board export subsidy is not—even though an across-the-board subsidy would probably be less distorting, and might even improve international efficiency.[8]

The question arises, why this stricter treatment of export subsidies than tariffs? The answer lies in *compelling* political realities. We are

---

8. Here is why. Consider first an economy with no tariffs or subsidies, with a freely flexible exchange rate, and only merchandise trade. (That is, there are no international services or capital flows.) Then a 10 percent across-the-board tax on imports and a 10 percent across-the-board subsidy to exports would have no distorting effect on trade (other than the administrative and nuisance costs). It would simply result in a 10 percent appreciation of the currency, leaving export and import prices and quantities unchanged in both the home and foreign countries. In other words, in the simple world postulated, export subsidies tend, *in equilibrium,* to cancel out the effects of import tariffs. If tariffs exist to begin with (as is the case), an across-the-board export subsidy *may* partially cancel them out, leading to greater efficiency.

This suggests a way a country might lower tariffs under a *pegged* exchange rate system. Instead of imposing import surcharges, a country with a balance of payments deficit might introduce an across-the-board export subsidy of say, 10 percent to improve its balance of payments. This could later be replaced with three moves: a 10 percent devaluation, an elimination of the subsidy, and a reduction of all tariffs by 10 percent. There would be no transition problem in reducing tariffs in such circumstances: foreign used to tariffs, and they represent the view that our market basically belongs to us. Subsidies, on the other hand, represent an unfair intrusion of foreigners upon our turf. We *cannot* make foreigners eliminate their tariffs on our goods. But it *is* within our power unilaterally to make foreigners eliminate their subsidies, or, even better, we may impose countervailing duties that eliminate their advantage and leave us with the tariff revenues to boot. A flat international prohibition on import tariffs would be useless; it would be widely ignored. A flat prohibition on export subsidies has teeth— it legitimizes foreign retaliation which removes the gain from subsidization. The international political problem is not how to gain leverage against subsidized exports. Rather, it is to circumscribe the definition of subsidies and the circumstances under which countervailing duties can be imposed, particularly in the case of domestic subsidies to production. As all countries have some subsidies to domestic industries, an unrestrained retaliation against such subsidies could lead to an escalation of tariffs.

In the United States, a countervailing duty law was passed in 1897, requiring the Secretary of the Treasury to assess CVD on dutiable goods benefiting from a "bounty or grant" on their exportation. In 1922, the law was extended to cover bounties or grants on production as well as on exportation. There was no injury test, and the countervailing duty was to be equal to the size of the foreign subsidy. (It was under this old law that the Wisconsin radiator manufacturer sued to force the Treasury to impose a countervailing duty on Canadian automotive exports in response to the duty remission programs of

---

goods would be no more competitive, because the tariff reduction would be offset by the devaluation of the currency.

This strategy has not in fact be used for several reasons. (1) Subsidies may lead to foreign countervailing duties, in which case they would make the balance of trade worse, not better. (2) Because of low short-run elasticities, export subsidies would make the trade balance worse in the short run, even in the absence of foreign countervailing. (The J-curve phenomenon arises because of problems on the export side. An import surcharge will improve the balance of payments, even in the short run.) Thus, the strategy is usable only when balance of payments problems are not severe, and the country can wait for a slow adjustment. (3) The granting of across-the-board subsidies would be costly to the Treasury. (4) The strategy is too complicated for the political process to handle.

1962–63.) In legislation passed in 1974, 1979, and 1984, a number of important amendments were made in the US CVD law, including the following:

• For imports from countries subscribing to the GATT Subsidies Code, an injury test is required prior to the imposition of countervailing duties (1979).

• Countervailing duties can be applied not only to dutiable but also nondutiable imports (1974).

• A number of changes were made in the procedural aspects of the law, limiting the discretion of the executive branch.[9]

In addition, a major change in US practices had already occurred in the Michelin tire case of 1973. Prior to that time, the practice of the Treasury had been to act only against export subsidies (Hufbauer and Shelton Erb 1984, pp. 90–91). Then, in an example of what Peter B. Feller (1969) has called "Mutiny Against the Bounty," a Canadian regional development grant to Michelin was found to be a countervailable subsidy. The transition to a broader definition of countervailable subsidy was facilitated in the Michelin tire case because about three-quarters of its output was destined for the United States.

The first two points were particularly significant for the current free trade talks between the United States and Canada. The first helped to limit potential disputes over subsidies, since a domestic industry must demonstrate injury before it gains the right to a CVD. (The Macdonald Commission [1985, p. 314] noted that the six cases where the United States imposed CVD on Canadian exports between 1975 and 1979 were all terminated when the injury test was introduced.) On the other hand, the applicability of CVD to nondutiable imports means that Canada faces a much more difficult problem in getting US commitments not to apply the CVD law than would have been the case before 1974. Prior to that date, a free trade agreement would have caused an elimination of CVD. Now, however, Canadian exemption from US CVD would not follow automatically from a free trade agreement, but would require explicit action on the part of the Congress—action which seems unlikely in the foreseeable future.

---

9. For details, see US House of Representatives, Ways and Means Committee, 1984, pp. 47–55.

In brief, US law focuses on the rights of domestic competitors. They have an unqualified right to a CVD equal to the amount of subsidy if the Department of Commerce[10] determines that a subsidy is being provided, either directly or indirectly, to the "manufacture, production, or exportation" of goods imported into the United States; and if, also, the USITC determines that the US industry is materially injured by the subsidized imports.

Much of US trade policy involves a balancing of the interests of producers against those of consumers. Although the interests of consumers are diffuse, their interests (as well as the interests of exporters) have been one of the reasons for US participation in various international negotiations to reduce tariffs. But the CVD law is quite specific: it safeguards the rights of producers against foreign subsidies; the interests of consumers are essentially irrelevant, once subsidies have been found to cause damage to domestic producers. In a world in which many tariffs are bound by international agreement, one way for producers to seek additional protection is to promote legislation to redefine whatever advantage foreign producers might have as a "subsidy." In fact, this process of redefining and broadening the concept of subsidies may be seen in some of the legislation recently proposed in the Congress—legislation that the administration has opposed.

What Is a Subsidy, and What Is Not?

Unfortunately, deciding what is a subsidy is not always simple. We may, however, begin with several relatively straightforward cases.

During the Tokyo Round, countries agreed that a number of provisions would be identified as *export* subsidies; these are included in an illustrative list provided in the Annex to the GATT Code on Subsidies and Countervailing Duties (hereafter referred to as the Subsidies Code).[11] The list includes items such as payments by the government to a firm or industry contingent upon export performance, and the grant by a government of export credits at interest rates below those the government itself has to pay for funds.

---

10. The Treasury's responsibility for enforcing the CVD law was transferred to the Commerce Department in 1980.
11. Reprinted in Hufbauer and Shelton Erb (1984, pp. 152–53).

Similarly, clear cases of *domestic* subsidy might be identified—for example, the outright payment of $x per unit of output, or the provision of loans at less than market rates as an incentive to initiate or expand production. Such domestic subsidies are treated differently from export subsidies under the GATT. Except for subsidies on "certain primary products," export subsidies are forbidden by the Subsidies Code (Article 9).[12] However, *domestic subsidies may legitimately be used to promote important social and policy objectives* (such as assistance to depressed regions); the Subsidies Code was not intended "to restrict the right of signatories to use such subsidies to achieve these and other important policy objectives" (Article 11). However, when using such domestic subsidies, countries are to seek to avoid causing damage to the industry of other countries. If they fail to do so, with the domestic industries of other countries suffering material injury, then those countries are allowed to impose CVD.

While these examples clearly constitute subsidies, care must be taken not to define subsidies so broadly that *any* foreign advantage is considered a subsidy. Subsidies are a politically charged issue; domestic competitors are entitled to redress once subsidies and material damage can be demonstrated, regardless of the overall loss or benefit of the nation. Foreign subsidies are considered inherently unsporting; they result in "unfair" competition. What is needed is a "level playing field." The problem is, how to define subsidies or unfairness in any but an arbitrarily subjective way. To continue the sports analogy, not all advantages are unfair; those who are swifter or more skillful tend to win; it would be absurd to weigh them down with bags of buckshot to give their opponents a "fair" (50-50) chance of winning. Bribing the referee is unfair competition; being able to run faster is not.

Similarly, in international trade, some advantages must be accepted as legitimate and fair, or the whole discussion degenerates into absurdities. Chile has relatively rich copper mines; it is one of the places where copper should be produced. It would make no economic sense to define the access of Chilean copper producers to their mines as an unfair advantage *ipso facto*, and impose countervailing duties to

---

12. There was a qualification: export credit practices in accordance with the guidelines of the Organization of Economic Cooperation and Development (OECD) were not to be considered a prohibited export subsidy (pararagraph k of the annex to the Subsidies Code).

raise the price of imported copper to whatever home-produced copper would cost in an importing nation. Such duties would represent the buckshot system of athletic handicapping. (In spite of its absurdity, this approach was at one time advocated by the proponents of the so-called "scientific" tariff—defined as the tariff that would bring the cost of foreign goods up to the domestic costs of production. The idea was an input to the "flexible tariff" of the Fordney–McCumber Act of 1922, and has survived in the EC's variable levy on agricultural imports.) It is precisely the differences among countries that lay the basis for mutually advantageous trade.

Nevertheless, not all advantages arising from access to cheap raw materials necessarily result in an efficient pattern of international trade. Under certain circumstances, the question may be raised as to whether the pricing of raw materials involves a subsidy that distorts the pattern of production. In April of 1986, when the "fast track" approach to trade negotiations with Canada barely survived a 10 to 10 tie in the Senate Finance Committee, one reason for negative votes was the complaint of the US lumber industry that they were being damaged by unfair, subsidized sales of timber to Canadian lumber producers. In October 1986, the Commerce Department issued a preliminary finding that Canadian softwood lumber benefited from a countervailable subsidy of 15 percent. At the end of December, Canada agreed to an export tax of 15 percent to avoid the imposition of a CVD, and to settle the dispute. (One incentive for Canada to settle was that it, rather than the US Treasury, reaps the tax revenues of about US$400 million.) This case illustrates some of the ambiguities surrounding subsidies.

SOFTWOOD LUMBER

The US softwood lumber industry's complaint was that Canadian provincial practices unfairly subsidize the Canadian lumber industry, primarily through artificially low "stumpage fees" on the removal of timber from government lands. The US industry further charged that Canadian overproduction has driven down the prices of US producers, putting many out of business. The CVD petition pointed out that, between 1975 and 1985, Canadian softwood lumber production increased by 105 percent, while US softwood lumber production rose only 19 percent.

The CVD petition repeated one of several years ago. At that time, the Commerce Department concluded that Canadian stumpage practices were not countervailable subsidies.

Because British Columbia produces about two-thirds of Canadian lumber exports destined for the United States, we will focus on the practices of that province. To calculate the stumpage fee on timber from public lands, British Columbia starts with the final price of the lumber (as sold in the United States), and deducts the costs of cutting the timber, transporting it and producing lumber, plus an allowance (of about 16 percent to 18 percent) for profit and risk. In other words, the stumpage fee is a *residual*, after profit and the costs of producing the lumber are subtracted. BC lumber producers are assured a steady supply of timber over extended periods of time at the appraised stumpage fee. Where the residual approach gives a negative calculation—as it has in recent years—there is a minimum stumpage fee equal to 3 percent of the value of the lumber.

Interestingly, the US government uses a similar procedure to appraise timber on public lands. However, standing timber is not sold at appraised prices, but is usually sold at auction, where the high bidder generally offers more than the appraised US price (and more than the Canadian stumpage fee). One source of difficulty in the US industry has been that lumber firms bid aggressively for stumpage rights several years ago when the market was relatively firm and rapid inflation was expected. In retrospect, they turn out to have bid too much.

Although the practices in the two countries differ, the BC system does not involve an obvious subsidy. Indeed, it makes economic sense in one important way: having raw material prices fluctuate in the face of fluctuating demand helps to ease cyclical pressures on producers, and reduces cyclical unemployment in the industry.

On the other hand, the BC system *might* be used to subsidize producers. For example, if the final price of lumber were underestimated, or if the costs of production were padded, then stumpage fees might be considered to be subsidized. In this regard, one question does seem to arise directly. The BC system tends to insulate the timber producers from some of the risks of business, since fluctuations in the price of lumber are automatically shifted back onto the stumpage fee.

This would suggest that the provision for risk should be somewhat smaller than would otherwise be the case. (Also, the provision for profits and risk is higher in British Columbia than in the US appraisal.)

It is beyond the scope of this study to try to provide an answer to the question of whether Canadian stumpage fees have represented a subsidy. However, it is possible to shed light on some of the issues.

First, there is one way it is *not* appropriate to address the question. The correct economic price for timber in Canada is not necessarily the same as in the United States; it does not make economic sense to define any difference between stumpage prices in the United States and Canada as *prima facie* evidence of a subsidy. That would be a variant on the "scientific tariff" approach. The appropriate economic price for raw materials is not the same in various countries—the price of Chilean copper ore should not necessarily be the same as the price of US ore, and the price of agricultural land in Texas or Iowa should not necessarily be the same as agricultural land in Japan.

Second, differences in raw material prices nevertheless do raise the issue of the efficient location of various stages in the productive process. Within an efficient market—whether a national market or a free trade area—there is a tendency for production to take place in the least costly location. This applies not only to final goods, but also earlier stages in the productive process. For example, computer components may be made in Minnesota or Texas, and steel in Pittsburgh or Gary, for inclusion in a car assembled in Detroit. Of course, transportation costs are part of the overall costs, and this means that production tends to be drawn toward markets or toward heavy and bulky raw material inputs.

For the lumber industry, the question arises as to whether each stage in the productive process is performed in the lowest-cost location. As long as Canadian provinces prohibit log exports (as British Columbia has done since 1906), American-based lumber mills are not permitted to compete for the business of converting those logs into lumber,[13] and thus there is a barrier to the efficient location of sawmills. One way of reducing frictions over stumpage fees would be to permit US

---

13. Since 1973, the United States also has also had a similar ban on the export of unprocessed logs from federal lands in the West, aimed at preventing shipments of logs to East Asia.

firms to buy stumpage rights and import the logs; that is, to make the timber available for export. Indeed, the export prohibition may be considered a major economic issue. The economic case against subsidies is that they distort the location of production. If Canada were to permit unhampered US access to the logs on the same terms as they are available to Canadian producers, then there would seem to be little ground for the US industry arguing that stumpage fees distort the location of sawmills. (Note that unhampered US access to Canadian logs would *not* involve Canada's "giving away" the logs; the provincial governments would charge US firms the market rate. The complaint of the US industry is that the provincial governments are selling the stumpage rights *too cheaply,* and in a preferential way to producers in Canada.)

It is, however, doubtful that Canada or the Canadian provinces will agree to free exports of logs or other raw materials as part of an overall free trade agreement. Many Canadians have a deep fear of losing control over their natural resources. The availability of cheap raw materials is considered an important public heritage, not to be lightly bargained away. (However, this principle is far from absolute. Canada has been an exporter of energy resources, such as oil and electricity—sometimes eagerly so. The point is that the export of natural resources is a politically sensitive subject.) A complicating factor is that export restrictions are applied by the province; they also apply to exports to other provinces within Canada.

The Canadian view of natural resources as a national (or provincial) heritage is certainly understandable. But it does mean that a fundamental "solution" to the resource issue is unlikely, in the sense of a meeting of minds between Canadians and Americans. Why do Canadians cherish their heritage of raw materials? One answer: the raw materials can be used as a way of providing jobs and prosperity to the Canadian people. But if jobs—in this case, sawmill jobs—are kept at home in Canada, with US firms being unable to compete on an equal footing for this stage in the productive process, then the US firms are likely to object to what they see as unfair Canadian competition. To put it somewhat differently: a country has an unqualified right to use its natural resources as it sees fit to satisfy the needs of its domestic population. But once it uses its resources as a basis for entering the export market, then it may meet objections from competing foreign producers, particularly if the resources are made available to domestic producers on a preferential basis. Firms in the importing country may feel that they are being unfairly blocked out of some stages in the productive process, regardless of how efficient they might be.

Third, if an open bidding system—with US firms being permitted to participate—is ruled out as politically unacceptable in Canada, the question remains as to what, if anything, can be said about the "correct" economic price. Specifically, is it appropriate to price timber as a residual—as the price of the lumber less sawmill and other production costs?

Under one set of circumstances, the answer is yes. If timber is a wasting resource—where forests are mature, with dead trees falling and rotting, and where present cutting does not reduce future harvests—then the opportunity cost of present cutting is zero; or, more precisely, it is limited to such current costs as the construction of roads. Any return that the government gets from stumpage fees (net of the government's current costs) represents a windfall; it is difficult to see how the government could be granting a subsidy if it is selling a resource for more than its opportunity cost. Indeed, pricing the timber as a residual—the cost of lumber less sawmill and other production costs—is the most obvious way of setting the stumpage fee. So long as timber is a wasting resource, there is no shortage, and therefore there is no need to limit cutting by raising the stumpage fee.

More generally, however, the cutting of timber today reduces the supply in the future. In this case, a simple residual formula is not appropriate; instead, the government should have a reservation price, to compensate for the cost in terms of less timber for future harvests. The calculation of the best reservation price is complicated, but here are some of the main considerations. If demand is already high enough so that more than the maximum sustainable yield is being cut (that is, young and small trees are taken, so that cutting 1,000 board feet now results in a decline of more than 1,000 board feet in future harvests), then the price should be raised enough to limit cutting (approximately)[14]

---

14. Two conflicting forces mean that the maximum sustainable yield does not represent *precisely* the correct rate of cutting. On the one hand, goods today are more valuable than goods tomorrow because of the productivity of capital and the positive real rate of interest. This works to make the optimal cut a bit more than the rate that will result in the maximum sustainable yield. On the other hand, trees may be cheaper to cut when they are large. Savings in the cost of harvesting provide an incentive to leave trees until they are larger; this works to make the optimal cut somewhat lower than the maximum sustainable rate.

to the maximum sustainable yield over the business cycle. An appropriate way for the government to allocate the scarce resource is to price it at whatever the market will bear, by auctioning off an amount (approximately) equal to the maximum sustainable yield. Even in the face of very high demand, cutting should not be allowed to exceed the maximum sustainable yield (by much) over the business cycle; conservation should be a high priority.

In the third, intermediate case, present cutting reduces future harvests, but by less than a 1:1 ratio. In this case, an intermediate system is appropriate, with purchasers bidding for stumpage rights. However, the quantity of those rights should be increased in response to high demand. The minimum stumpage fee should be at least enough to cover the costs of maintaining the forests—reforestation, fire control, the maintenance of logging roads, and so forth.

Currently, BC practices approximate the first case; US practices the third, intermediate case. The Commerce Department's preliminary determination of a countervailable subsidy depended partly on the finding that the stumpage fees were not sufficiently high to cover the imputed cost of standing timber (1986b, pp. 21–23). The implication is that the Canadian provinces cannot properly be classified as a "first case," with timber being a wasting resource. The evidence on this point does not, however, seem to be unambiguous. For example, in an earlier study, the USITC (1985, p. 9) reported that a large portion of Canadian timber is in old-growth stands that are "being destroyed by insects and diseases that eventually will leave much of the timber worthless." This would suggest that Canada does, indeed, lie in the first category; if so, this would legitimize the Canadian procedure of treating stumpage as a residual (although it would not necessarily legitimize the particular cost estimates used in the Canadian system). In short, the subsidy case is a difficult judgment call, which might have gone either way. This is scarcely surprising, because it has in fact gone both ways—a countervailable subsidy having been found in 1986, but not in the earlier investigation in 1983.

LUMBER: THE "GENERAL AVAILABILITY" TEST

A major reason for the 1986 reversal has to do with the test of "specificity" or "general availability." As interpreted by the Commerce Department, a subsidy is countervailable if it is enjoyed by one or a few specific industries; it is not countervailable if it is generally available to all comers, on a nonpreferential basis. Thus, for example, a general government subsidy to all industries to supplement the wages of low-wage workers would not be a countervailable subsidy.

In 1983, Canadian stumpage practices were found to be not countervailable because they were judged to be "generally available." Low stumpage fees were enjoyed by a number of industries—lumber and wood products, pulp and paper, and furniture. In its preliminary finding of a countervailable subsidy in 1986, the Department of Commerce found several reasons for changing its 1983 decision, of which two are of special interest. First was an evolution and tightening of the department's interpretation of general availability, resulting in part from a court decision in the Mexican Carbon Black case. Second was a factual finding—that the number of different users of stumpage was fewer than found in 1983. Specifically, Commerce (1986b, p. 17) found

one undisputed fact: furniture manufacturers own negligible rights, if they hold any rights at all, to stumpage in any of the four relevant provinces. Thus, contrary to our determination in *Softwood Products* [1983], the industries actually using provincial stumpage do not include the furniture manufacturing industries.

This point—that a CVD on about \$3 billion in Canadian lumber exports to the United States should rest in an important way on whether furniture producers do or do not also have access to cheap stumpage—seems bizarre. It is not clear what difference it would make if furniture manufacturers also cut trees. It may be that hard cases not only make bad law; they may also make bad economics. Nevertheless, the general idea—that broadly available subsidies should not be countervailed—does make sense. A subsidy available to all should have little effect on resource allocation, and resource misallocation provides the major economic argument against subsidies. The problem is where to draw the line in a quasi-legal proceeding, in which general subsidies escape countervail while specific subsidies do not. The Department of Commerce is aware of this problem; it notes (1986b, p.12) that general availability is "one of the more controversial aspects" of the CVD law.

LUMBER: HAVE "SUBSIDIES" BEEN THE PROBLEM?

The lumber case shows just how slippery the concept of "countervailable subsidy" can be. Perhaps we should begin to think of alternatives to the CVD approach in such ambiguous cases, involving natural resources. There may be a tendency to consider any deviation from US practices (or prices) as "unfair subsidies." Not only does the charge of unfairness raise the political heat, and make compromise more difficult. It also raises fears in Canada that the United States may, with its CVD policy, attempt to force Canada to adopt domestic policies similar to those of the United States—a fear expressed by Canadian International Trade Minister Patricia Carney in discussing lumber. Yet resource management may be quite controversial within each country, and there is no compelling reason for all countries to adopt similar policies. The need for conservation may, for example, vary widely among nations. Presumably, the major problem is not the specific policies followed by exporting nations, but rather the disruptions and damages suffered by the domestic industry in the United States, and how these damages are weighed against the cost to consumers when the United States imposes levies on imports or pressures Canada to impose export taxes. One option would be to avoid CVD proceedings in such resource-based cases, and move toward an escape clause type action instead, without attribution of fault to the foreign government. This would be particularly appropriate where the case for countervailing duties is as ambiguous as it seems in the stumpage case (as illustrated by the quite different decisions in 1983 and 1986).

The case for rethinking the CVD law is strengthened because it is not clear that Canadian subsidies have been the *source* of the US lumber industry's problem, even though the industry *has* faced severe competitive pressures from Canada. Suppose, for the moment, that there is no doubt that Canadian provinces do, in fact, subsidize stumpage. Suppose, further, that the present system were replaced with competitive bidding, resulting in higher stumpage fees and the elimination of the subsidies. So long as the same annual average cut were allowed in Canada, and so long as the prohibition on log exports remained, the switch to competitive bidding might provide no relief to US lumber mills. Approximately the same amount of lumber would be produced in Canada, and approximately the same amount would be available for export. Canadian lumber producers would be less well off. They would receive a smaller windfall from the provincial governments; there would be a redistribution of economic rents within Canada. But the US industry would be no better off; Canadian lumber would still be capturing a sizeable share of the US market. In other words, the US industry has faced a problem primarily because of the large *quantity* of timber available for cutting in Canada, not because of the *price* of the standing timber. Subsidized Canadian lumber may have caused harm to the US industry, but it was not the *subsidy* that was the cause of injury. Rather, it was the *quantity* of Canadian lumber available for export.

Thus, the CVD law seems designed to deal with quite a different problem, where foreign subsidies encourage greater production and flood the US domestic market with more and more imports. This is most likely to be the case in manufacturing or other industries that use nonspecific factors and can readily expand. It is not the case in the lumber industry, where the allowable annual cut is the key determinant of the quantity of output and exports.

The BC procedures for setting and enforcing the amount of timber cutting may have been one source of difficulty for the US industry. Specifically, British Columbia has a "cut-it-or-lose-it" provision. Any firm that takes less than 90 percent of its allowable cut over a five-year period has its future cut reduced. This provision tends to keep production stable in Canada in the face of fluctuating prices and market conditions. To keep their cut for the future, Canadian lumber producers may be induced to produce more than they otherwise would. This pushes cyclical pressures off on US producers. Earlier, we argued that the clearest problems arise, not so much from steady, long-term subsidies, but from steps by foreign nations that unload cyclical disturbances and adjustment problems on the US industry. Because the BC "cut-it-or-lose-it" provision tends to do just that, it is perhaps the most questionable aspect of BC lumber policy. (However, it has not been one of the issues on which the CVD case has turned. Furthermore, this provision is not intrinsically unfair; similar provisions are used in the northwestern United States.)

Cyclical problems for US lumber producers have been intensified not only by the BC "cut-it-or-lose-it" provision, but also by the US fixed-bidding system, which represented a gamble for the bidders. When lumber prices fell unexpectedly, the firms could be squeezed severely, as they were at the beginning of the 1980s. Fortunately, changes were made in the system in 1982 to reduce such risks: stumpage prices were adjusted to compensate, at least in part, for changes in the price of lumber. There is much to be said for this modification. In an industry where demand fluctuates strongly over the business cycle, a transfer of pressures back to the prices of raw material is appropriate.

(Even though forest-management policies in both countries have tended to concentrate cyclical instabilities in the US industry, this cyclical effect has not been strong. It is easiest to find in the period prior to 1982, when the US stumpage prices were modified. Between 1977 and 1982, US lumber consumption declined. Canadian lumber exports participated in the decline, but less than proportionately: while US lumber production was falling 24 percent, imports from Canada fell only 13 percent. The percentage of the US market filled by Canadian lumber rose from 24.4 percent to 27.5 percent.)

LUMBER: A SUMMARY

To summarize the main points raised regarding lumber:

• Differences in stumpage practices, or in stumpage prices between the United States and Canada are not *prima facie* evidence of a subsidy.

• Prohibitions on the export of logs means that American lumber mills can be at a disadvantage, even where they saw lumber as cheaply as Canadian mills. But, while freedom to export might be a way of dealing with complaints that natural resources are subsidized, it seems most unlikely to be acceptable in Canada. This is particularly so for logs; there are prohibitions on log exports even among Canadian provinces.

• One reason for the reversal between 1983 and 1986 depended on the interpretation of "general availability." Specifically, the Commerce Department in 1986 found that Canadian furniture companies were not significant users of stumpage rights.

• The general availability test makes sense, as an input into CVD decisions. Nevertheless, it has been applied in a curious manner in the lumber case. It is not clear what difference it would make to the US lumber industry if Canadian furniture manufacturers also used stumpage rights.

• Even though US lumber producers may have suffered injury because of subsidized Canadian exports, it was the *quantity* of Canadian lumber available for exports that was the problem, not whether the lumber was or was not actually subsidized.

• The CVD law seems designed to deal with industries that use nonspecific inputs, and which can expand rapidly in response to subsidies. It does not seem designed for industries such as lumber, where the amount of available timber is the key determinant of output and exports.

• The BC "cut-it-or-lose-it" provision tended to concentrate cyclical fluctuations in the US lumber industry. It was perhaps the most problematic aspect of BC lumber policy, although it was not an important issue in the CVD proceedings.

Subsidies and Social Policies

The lumber case has confirmed Canadian fears that the application of US law may change in unpredictable ways. However, the idea of general availability, and its recent application by the United States, should be reassuring in another sense. One of the concerns often expressed in Canada is that the US CVD law will be used to reach into Canada and interfere with Canadian social policies, such as health insurance, unemployment insurance, and regional development grants. Actual cases—most notably, Michelin, but also the recent fish and lumber cases—suggest that regional development grants do risk US countervailing action. But programs such as unemployment and health insurance do not—at least they do not so long as they are generally available across industries.

Unemployment insurance came up explicitly in the recent CVD case against Atlantic groundfish. ("Groundfish"—such as cod, haddock, flounder and sole—are so called because they live near the seabed.)

One of the complaints of the US fishing industry was that the Canadian Unemployment Insurance Act represented a subsidy. The point at issue was not the countervailability of the general unemployment insurance program; as it is *generally available* to Canadian workers, it is not countervailable. The question, rather, was whether special provisions of the Canadian law, applying only to self-employed fishermen, represented a subsidy to that *particular* industry. While the terms applied to self-employed fishermen were not identical to those available to contract workers, the Commerce Department found that they were better in some respects, and inferior in others. It accordingly concluded (1986a, p. 10059) that "unemployment insurance provided to self-employed fishermen is not provided on preferential terms and therefore is not countervailable." Thus, although a number of subsidies were found, and CVD duties of 5.8 percent imposed, unemployment insurance was not in the list of countervailable subsidies.

Regional development grants were, however, included as countervailable subsidies in the groundfish case, reaffirming the finding in the Michelin tire case (under which CVD ranging from 1.2 percent to 2.5 percent were imposed between 1973 and 1982). Such regional development grants are countervailable since they apply only to specific depressed areas, and are not generally available. Because of the emphasis on such grants in Canada, this is an aspect of US CVD law of particular interest north of the border.

Trade Remedy Laws: How Might They Be Applied in a Free Trade Area?

Within a national market, trade remedy laws are not applied; there are no countervailing or antidumping duties within the United States. This is not because of an absence of subsidies or dumping. For example, states and localities frequently provide tax breaks or other financial incentives to new plants, and companies sometimes "dump" surpluses into cut-rate channels, particularly at the end of production runs. Nevertheless, duties among states or localities are prohibited, in order to provide a large, unimpeded internal market. Within national boundaries, countries either deal with dumping or subsidy problems in ways other than through duties—for example, the use of antitrust or other business law to regulate the freedom of companies to engage in multiple pricing—or they live with the problems. Thus, states learn to live with the competition from other states for new plants. This is not necessarily optimal; states and localities as a whole might be better off if they all agreed not to engage in competitive bidding for new plants. But the internal market within the United States still works well. Similarly, the internal US market works quite well in the absence of escape clause actions. When the textile industry was migrating to the South some decades ago, New England was given no protection from Southern textiles, even though the migration clearly caused substantial short-term injury in New England.

This raises the question of whether the United States and Canada might agree to eliminate dumping, subsidy, and escape clause actions against one another in the event of a free trade agreement. Hope for exemption from US "contingent protection" has been expressed in Canada; it would be the simplest, and most comprehensive, way of achieving assured access to the US market.

A bilateral exemption from trade remedy laws would be extremely difficult to achieve. When the US-Israeli free trade agreement was being negotiated, the question was raised of an Israeli exemption from US trade remedy laws. It was a nonstarter. Yet the Israeli case was much simpler than the Canadian: Israel poses a much smaller threat of injury to US industry, and Israel can count on a more sympathetic hearing in Congress. There seems little chance that Congress would agree to a blanket exemption of Canada in the near future unless there is a truly comprehensive agreement, including firm commitments on subsidies. (If free trade had been negotiated before 1974, Canada would have been automatically exempted from CVD action, since it applied only to dutiable imports at that time. If a free trade agreement had already been in place, it might have been possible to continue the exemption for Canada when CVD was made applicable to nondutiable imports in the 1974 legislation. But that represents an opportunity lost for Canada.) On the other side, Canada seems reluctant to consider an elimination of its own contingent protection, particularly antidumping duties.[15] Because of the experience with the Auto Pact, it is out

15. Department of External Affairs (1985, p. 25): "[T]he relatively greater exposure of Canadian production to US import competition could require the retention of some form of anti-dumping procedures. One option for consideration would be the development of a separate bilateral regime." For a nongovernmental view that antidumping duties should be retained, see the study by Richard G. Lipsey and Murray G. Smith (1985, p. 157).

of the question to have an asymmetric arrangement, with the United States exempting Canada while Canada maintains its own trade remedy laws.

The negotiators are therefore likely to have to settle for a more limited agreement. The place to start is with a less ambitious question: What, if anything, can be done to limit the application of trade remedy laws, or to make them more predictable, or to reduce the need for remedies? With regard to the key issue of subsidies and CVD, several possibilities might be considered.

A RELATIVELY UNAMBITIOUS PACKAGE

A minimal package might have several components:

• a Canadian elimination of the *auto rebates* and a commitment not to reintroduce them

• an understanding that new trade remedy cases would go first to a *bilateral commission;* an effort would be made to reach a negotiated settlement at an early stage

• an increase in the *de minimis* provision, as it applies to the partner country.[16]

At present, a CVD is not imposed if the foreign subsidy is less than 0.5 percent of the value of the product; this might be increased to 2.0 percent or 2.5 percent for Canada. It is hard to see how a small subsidy of, say, 2 percent could cause substantial distortion of international trade. Such a threshold would have been almost—but not quite—high enough to eliminate the CVD in the famous Michelin case; at its maximum, the CVD was 2.51 percent. The higher *de minimis* would eliminate CVD for *modest* regional development programs, provided they were not used in combination with other subsidies.

---

16. The preferential increase in the *de minimis* might be considered a violation of the MFN approach of the GATT. However, it is consistent with the logic of Article XXIV: once countries decide to enter a free trade agreement, the more completely they eliminate barriers between one another, the better, even though they are not extending the benefits to outside countries.

AN INTERMEDIATE PACKAGE

In addition to the above items, a more ambitious package might include:

- An agreement to exempt each other from any future extension of trade remedy laws. For example, CVDs are not now applicable to generally available subsidies, such as a broadly based investment tax credit. The continued exemption of such generally available subsidies might be included in a bilateral agreement.[17]

- Some progress on narrowing the differences over acceptable and unacceptable practices. That is, there would be an extension of the approach begun in GATT, specifying practices that are acceptable (such as rebates of indirect taxes) and those that are not (export subsidies). A gray area might also be identified—subsidies that would be acceptable, up to a specified limit. Regional development grants would be a good candidate for this category. Research and development grants might be put in the white (acceptable) or gray category.

- A further increase in the threshold level, to perhaps 4 percent or 5 percent. (At this level, it presumably would no longer be called a "*de minimis*" provision.)

- An agreement to eliminate unacceptable practices, and to limit "gray area" subsidies (including regional development grants) to no more than the threshold of 4 percent or 5 percent.

The last three items are an inseparable package. The Congress would be unlikely to agree to a major increase in the threshold without a Canadian commitment to limit its subsidy programs. On the other hand, it would be politically difficult in Canada to agree to limit subsidy programs, without some relief from the application of the US countervailing duty law.

The negotiation of this package will not be easy. On both sides of the border, perceptions differ sharply regarding acceptable practices— the duty rebates for the auto industry illustrate just how sharply. Nevertheless, the time may be ripe for an effort to separate the acceptable from the unacceptable. Some years ago, during the negotiation of the GATT Subsidies Code, Canada and the European

---

17. The standstill proposal has been made by Lipsey and Smith (1985, pp. 152–53).

Community were unenthusiastic when the United States suggested that subsidies be defined more precisely. Canada is now interested in a more precise definition, as a way of reducing the uncertainties in the the application of the US CVD law.

With this package, each country would retain the right to decide unilaterally whether its industry was being damaged by countervailable subsidies. However, as in the "unambitious package," a bilateral commission would be included in the decision-making loop. This might permit a mutually acceptable solution at an early stage—in contrast to the lumber negotiations, which took place "under the gun" of an impending final decision. Furthermore, if both sides kept to the agreement, and subsidies were held below the threshold level, then CVD would not be applied to the exports of the other country.

AN AMBITIOUS APPROACH

A more ambitious approach would be similar to that in the European Community, where countervailing duties are not permitted in trade among member countries. Instead, there is a supranational regulation of subsidies. The EC Commission can review subsidies of the various members, to identify those that distort competition. Legal action can be taken in the European Court of Justice if the subsidizing country persists.

To get to such an ambitious result, it would be highly desirable to go through the process in the second, intermediate package, agreeing on lists of acceptable and unacceptable practices. The subsidy issue has been much too contentious to be simply dumped, without guidelines, into the hands of an international tribunal. It is worse than useless to establish a tribunal whose decisions are likely to be defied. Although it is difficult at this stage to be optimistic that the ambitious result can be achieved, the process of defining acceptable and unacceptable practices might be the place to start. *If* the negotiators can make solid progress on that topic, then they might raise their sights, and aim for the the more ambitious outcome.

OTHER OPTIONS

In addition to the above three packages, the CVD issue can be approached in other ways. One would be to apply CVD only to *differential subsidies.* CVDs are based on the complaint that subsidies distort trade, and represent unfair competition. Competition is not, however, unfair if there are equivalent subsidies on both sides of the border. In their recent study, Richard G. Lipsey and Murray Smith (1985, p. 153) suggest that CVD be applicable only to the extent that subsidies in the exporting country exceed subsidies to the same industry at home.

Logically, this is a forceful argument. Equal subsidies represent a level playing field; they do not distort the relative competitive positions of foreign and domestic producers. The focus on differential subsidies would help to correct a common misperception, that the United States is pure in this regard and is the innocent victim of unfair foreign practices.

But, in spite of the forceful case that might be made for limiting CVD to differential subsidies, I have not included this option in the above packages, primarily because of the difficulties of applying it in practice. Suppose, for example, that a community in Nova Scotia outbids a location in Ohio for a tire plant—as happened some years ago in the Michelin case. What is the differential subsidy? The amount by which Nova Scotia outbid Ohio? The total subsidy going to the Canadian location, since the proffered US subsidy was not accepted? The subsidy going to the Canadian plant, less the *highest* subsidy actually received by any US tire plant? Or should we instead subtract the *average* subsidy to US tire plants? Or just the *lowest* subsidy to any US tire plant?

Another approach—also suggested by Lipsey and Smith (1985, p. 153)—would be to apply CVD only to the *net subsidy* in regional development cases. The net subsidy would be calculated by deducting the increased costs of establishing a plant away from the prime national location. Such deductions would leave foreign competitors facing undistorted competition; that is, the competition that they would already face from the best national location. Thus, regional development grants would not be countervailable if they resulted in a relocation of industry within a country; they would only be countervailable to the extent that they gave a firm a net competitive advantage in export markets.

Prior to 1979, the US Treasury in fact calculated net subsidies for CVD purposes; among other deductions was the increased cost of locating away from the prime national location. Although the Trade

Agreements Act of 1979 retained the idea of a net subsidy, the Senate Committee Report specifically disallowed such increased regional costs as one of the permissible deductions. Thus, an agreement on regional subsidies would represent a backtracking by Congress. However, because it has proved workable in the past, it might possibly be considered part of an intermediate package, if substantial progress is made toward an overall trade agreement.

Because the CVD and subsidy issue is so contentious, the chances of an acceptance of any of the three packages is increased if it is included in a broader agreement, containing elements attractive to both sides. Some of the other important issues in the US-Canadian trade negotiations are considered in the next chapter.

ANNEX 4A Samples of Canadian Automotive Duty Remission Orders

Registration
SI/85-49   3 April, 1985

FINANCIAL ADMINISTRATION ACT

Honda Remission Order, 1984

P.C. 1985-810 14 MARCH, 1985

Her Excellency the Governor General in Council, considering that it is in the public interest to make the annexed remission Order, is pleased hereby, on the recommendation of the Minister of Regional Industrial Expansion, the Minister of Finance and the Treasury Board, pursuant to section 17* of the Financial Administration Act, to revoke the Honda Remission Order, 1980, made by Order in Council P.C. 1980-2066 of 31st July, 1980** and to make the annexed Order respecting the remission of customs duty on automobiles of Honda Canada Inc.

ORDER RESPECTING THE REMISSION OF CUSTOMS DUTY ON AUTOMOBILES OF HONDA CANADA INC.

Short Title
1. This Order may be cited as the *Honda Remission Order, 1984.*

AUTHOR'S NOTE: *Full English-language text,* Canada Gazette, *part II, vol. 119, no. 7 (3 April 1985), p. 1654.*
* S.C. 1980-81-82-83, c. 170, s.4
** SI/80-150, 1980 *Canada Gazette* Part II, p. 2756

Interpretation
2. In this Order,

"automobile" means a four-wheeled passenger automobile having a seating capacity for not more than ten persons;

"Company" means Honda Canada Inc.;

"Canadian automotive components" means original equipment, parts and accessories or parts thereof for vehicles, except tires and tubes in quantities in excess of those used on or similar to those used on the vehicles imported by the Company during a twelve month period, that are manufactured in Canada by or on behalf of the Company and exported to any country;

"Canadian value added" means
> (a) in respect of Canadian automotive components produced by the Company, or any subsidiary wholly-owned corporation or subsidiary controlled corporation of the Company and exported, the aggregate of
>> (i) the costs of producing those Canadian automotive components and the depreciation and capital allowances that would be included in the calculation of Canadian value added in accordance with the *Tariff Item 95000 (Entry of Motor Vehicles) Regulations* if the Canadian automotive components were vehicles, and
>> (ii) the cost of transporting those Canadian automotive components to the Canadian border, and
>
> (b) in respect of Canadian automotive components produced by a company other than a corporation described in paragraph (a) and exported, the producer's selling price of the Canadian automotive components and the cost of transporting those Canadian automotive components to the Canadian border less the duty paid value of imported goods used in the production thereof and any foreign charges applicable thereon;

"twelve month period" means a period beginning on August 1, 1984 and ending on July 31, 1985 and any subsequent twelve month period beginning on August 1;

"value for duty" has the same meaning as in the *Customs Act;*

"vehicle" means an automobile, specified commercial vehicle or bus as defined in the *Motor Vehicles Tariff Order, 1965.*

Remission of Customs Duty
3. Subject to section 5, remission in the amount set out in section 4 is granted of the duty specified in Schedule A to the *Customs Tariff* paid or payable in respect of automobiles manufactured by Honda Motor Co., Ltd., Japan, or by any subsidiary company of Honda Motor Co., Ltd., Japan, that are imported or taken out of warehouse by the Company.

4. The remission granted by section 3 shall be 70 per cent of the customs duty in respect of automobiles imported or taken out of warehouse during a twelve month period.

Conditions
5. (1) A remission granted under this Order is on condition that a claim is made to the Minister of National Revenue.

(2) Remission shall not be granted under this Order in respect of any automobile imported or taken out of warehouse during a twelve month period if by so importing or taking out of warehouse of that automobile by the Company the aggregate value for duty of all automobiles imported or taken out of warehouse for which remission is claimed during that period exceeds the Canadian value added of Canadian automotive components exported during that period.

(3) In determining the Canadian value added of Canadian automotive components for the purpose of subsection (2), there shall not be included in the determination those Canadian automotive components in respect of which there has been granted a remission of customs duty under any Order that contains a Canadian value added requirement.

Security
6. The Company shall, to guarantee the performance of the conditions on which remission is granted under this Order, furnish the Minister of National Revenue with a guarantee bond or other security in an amount equal to the customs duty remitted to the Company during a twelve month period.

Reports
7. The Company shall submit to the Minister of Regional Industrial Expansion such reports in such form and manner as may be required by the Minister for the purposes of this Order.

Honda Remission Order, 1985-1

P.C. 1986-637 13 MARCH, 1986

Her Excellency the Governor General in Council . . . is pleased hereby
. . . to revoke the Honda Remission Order, 1984, made by Order in
Council P.C. 1985-810 of 14th March, 1985, and to make the annexed
Order respecting the remission of customs duty on automobiles of
Honda Canada Inc.

. . . .

Interpretation
2. In this Order. . . .

"Canadian automotive components" means original equipment,
parts and accessories or parts thereof for vehicles, except tires and
tubes in quantities in excess of those used on or similar to those
used on the vehicles imported by the Company during a period,
that are produced in Canada by or on behalf of the Company and
exported to any country.

. . . .

Remissions of Customs Duty
. . . .

4. The remission granted . . . shall be in an amount equal to
(a) in the case of automobiles, 100 per cent of the customs duty
paid or payable in respect of automobiles imported or taken out of
warehouse during a period; and

(b) in the case of automobile parts, 100 per cent of the customs
duty that would have been paid or would be payable in respect of
automobile parts imported or taken out of warehouse during a
period if the customs duty had been or were calculated at a rate
equal to the applicable rate of customs duty specified in Schedule
A to the *Customs Tariff* for automobiles. . . .

AUTHOR'S NOTE: *Excerpts from* Canada Gazette *part II, vol. 120, no. 7 (2 April 1986), p.
1377.*

Honda Remission Order, 1980

P.C. 1980-2066 31 JULY, 1980

His Excellency the Governor General in Council . . . is pleased hereby
to make the annexed Order respecting the remission of Customs Duty
and Sales Tax on automobiles of Canadian Honda Motor Limited.

. . . .

Interpretation
2. In this Order, . . .

"Canadian automotive components" means parts and accessories
or parts thereof for vehicles, except tires and tubes, that are
manufactured in Canada by or on behalf of Honda, and exported
to any country, except the customs territory of the United States
including its insular possessions. . . .

AUTHOR'S NOTE: *Excerpts from* Canada Gazette *part II, vol. 114, no. 15 (13 August 1980),
p. 2756.*

Volkswagen Remission Order 1978

P.C. 1978-2658 23 AUGUST, 1978

His Excellency the Governor General in Council, . . . is pleased hereby
to make the annexed Order respecting the remission of Customs Duty
and Sales Tax on automobiles of Volkswagen Canada Ltd.

. . . .

Interpretation
2. In this Order, . . .

"Canadian automotive components" means parts and accessories
or parts thereof for vehicles, except tires and tubes, that are
manufactured in Canada by or on behalf of Volkswagen and exported
to any country. . . .

AUTHOR'S NOTE: *Excerpts from* Canada Gazette *part II, vol. 112, no. 17 (13 September
1978), p. 3628.*

5   Coverage of a Free Trade Accord

The current round of bilateral negotiations will, of course, address the question of tariffs and other barriers to commodity trade. Will it be possible not only to agree to reduce barriers on selected goods, but also to go much further, and *eliminate* barriers on *substantially all* products? This would keep the agreement within Article XXIV of the General Agreement on Tariffs and Trade (GATT), and would avoid a conflict between an agreement with Canada and adherence to the most-favored-nation (MFN) principle. The first topic of this chapter will be the commodity coverage of an agreement, and products where exceptions might be made. We will then turn to nontariff topics on the negotiating table—items such as national, provincial, and state procurement policies, services, investment, and adjustment to a free trade area. Finally, we will look at a rather technical subject: rules of origin and the problem of tariff drawbacks on inputs imported from third countries.

Commodity Coverage: Possible Exceptions

In entering a free trade negotiation, the appropriate starting place is to include as wide a range of products as possible. Once exceptions are allowed, the whole idea of a comprehensive agreement may begin to unravel. Furthermore, there is a very good economic rationale behind GATT Article XXIV, as explained in chapter 2: if countries are allowed to pick and choose freely among commodities, they may naturally make bilateral deals in industries where efficiency-reducing trade diversion will be large, and avoid efficiency-increasing tariff cuts. In addition, there are likely to be disagreements over the specific industries to be covered, with each side fearful that the other will gain the major advantage.

Nevertheless, possible exceptions must be addressed explicitly. It will not be feasible to include everything in an agreement. The possibility of exclusion arises in two particular areas—agriculture and industries under pressure.

AGRICULTURE

The strongest case for exceptions can be made in agriculture. The sad case of the European Community's common agricultural policy—with its high costs, high subsidies, and disruptive effects on world trade— suggests that the inclusion of agriculture in a free trade grouping does not necessarily promote efficiency. Within a bilateral agreement between the United States and Canada, it is hard to see how unrestricted trade could be allowed in all agricultural products *without fundamental changes in the price support programs*—programs that are unlikely to be changed to promote bilateral trade. GATT Article XXIV (8b) recognizes an exception to the general rule of eliminating barriers to substantially all trade: countries may retain import restrictions on agricultural or fish products as part of a system of supply management or domestic price support. The European Free Trade Association (EFTA) set a precedent, eliminating tariffs and quotas on almost all industrial products, but with only selective coverage for agricultural, fish, and food products. For the United States and Canada, the question is: which, if any, agricultural products should be covered by a free trade agreement?

One product which rather clearly should not be covered is wheat. Here, the major issue for the two countries is not how to eliminate barriers between them, but rather how to gain greater access to overseas markets while limiting the use of subsidies. Neither country is likely to agree to the changes in domestic policies that would be a necessary precondition for unrestricted passage of wheat across the border. On the other hand, an agreement might include a number of agricultural products in which a fair amount of trade between the countries already occurs—for example, beef, pork, and fruits and vegetables. Because of the prevalence of agricultural subsidies, some understanding on subsidies would be necessary if these sectors were to be included. (Canadian hogs are subject to a US countervailing duty, while the Canadian government has made a preliminary CVD duty finding against US corn.)

In a recent study, Andrew Schmitz and Colin Carter concluded that free trade in agricultural products would be unlikely to result in large gains inefficiency (1987). Gains are most likely to come from expanded trade in livestock, and perhaps also in eggs, poultry, and dairy products.

The most interesting of these may be eggs, where Canadian prices are high as a result of provincial egg marketing boards which regulate output, allocate production quotas among numerous small producers, and severely restrict competition among provinces. An inclusion of eggs within the free trade package would require major modifications or abolition of provincial marketing boards; as they stand, they block both international and interprovincial trade. With an opening of international and interprovincial competition, Canadian egg producers would come under significant pressure from much lower cost eggs from the United States, although these short-term pressures might be eased by a gradual transition to free trade. In the long run, Canadian egg production could not survive in its present form—to be competitive, Canadian producers would have to operate on a much larger scale. If free trade is to come in this industry, the most delicate negotiations will occur between the Canadian government and the provinces, not between the two national governments. The central question is whether Canada will use the bilateral negotiations as an opportunity to move toward a more rational internal system. The same question arises in a number of other agricultural products, where provincial nontariff barriers have led to a balkanization of Canadian agriculture, and a shift away from the most efficient regional pattern of production. Schmitz and Carter point to government programs aimed at provincial self-sufficiency as the cause of the decline in the Western provinces' share of Canadian hog production, from 46 percent in 1971 to 30 percent in 1984.

In the chicken industry, US producers of broilers also operate on a much larger scale, and at substantially lower costs, than Canadian producers. Again, free trade would require larger-scale operations on the part of Canadian producers who hoped to survive. In the dairy industry, milk marketing orders mean that the interstate flow of milk is as highly regulated in the United States as the interprovincial flow is in Canada. Freer movement of dairy products would require either a substantial modification, or a difficult fitting together, of two complex domestic systems.

INDUSTRIES UNDER PRESSURE

Industries under intense competitive pressure—such as textiles and steel—might also press for exemption from a bilateral free trade agreement. There are, however, good reasons not to exempt these products.

First, although adjustments in such industries are often painful, they can add to the long-run efficiency of the economy. For example, within the United States, a major attempt to prevent the migration of textiles from New England to the South would have reduced efficiency. Second, much of the adjustment will occur within industries, rather than between industries; there is no prospect that the US textile industry will wipe out the Canadian industry, or vice versa—although not all firms are guaranteed survival. Again, reorganization within industries can contribute to efficiency. This increase in efficiency would strengthen the ability of North American producers to compete with imports from overseas. Third, a gradual elimination of tariffs and nontariff barriers would ease the process of transition. Fourth, the move to free trade should be accompanied by domestic adjustment assistance in each country, which would further cushion the risks to firms and workers in industries under pressure. Finally, in cases of severe disruption, escape clause actions would still be possible; the retention of the escape clause would seem to be a preferable solution to the exemption of troubled industries altogether.[1]

Government Procurement

One aspect of an open trading regime is "national treatment" of the goods of other countries; once the tariff is paid, national treatment

---

1. In his recent paper, Sperry Lea of the National Planning Association (1987) recommends that exceptions to free trade be permitted only in agriculture.

means that they are granted an equal ability to compete with domestic goods. However, all countries fall far short of national treatment in government procurement. Canada and the United States have preferences for domestic goods, both in federal purchases and in provincial or state purchases.

In free trade negotiations, one important question is whether nondiscriminatory access to government procurement can be achieved. For example, can the "Buy America" act become a "Buy North America" act? (In the free trade agreement with Israel [Article 15], the United States waived all Buy America restrictions on purchases of $50,000 or more.) For Canada, this is an important negotiating objective; Canada has been particularly eager to gain access to contracts for subway cars under the US Surface Transportation Assistance Act, a federal-state cost-sharing program that has been 80 percent funded by the federal government. One problem is how to bring states, and particularly provinces, along in a more open procurement system. Many states and provinces have substantial preferences for local suppliers. That is, they discriminate not only against suppliers from other countries, but also against suppliers from other states or provinces. A starting point would be to provide national treatment to firms of the other country in federal and federally supported contracts; as a condition for federal financial assistance (in urban transit, for example), state and local governments might be required to provide equal treatment for the suppliers of the partner nation. More difficult will be to reduce local preferences for contracts financed entirely by states and provinces. Particularly in Canada, where provinces play a more important role than do the American states, provincial preferences reduce efficiency within the nation. As free trade discussions progress between the two national governments, the parallel discussions between the Canadian government and the provinces can make an important contribution to the reduction of trade barriers.

A related matter has to do with alcoholic beverages, where the provinces are not the final purchasers, but have control over what is offered for sale, and under what terms. In many instances, strong preferences are given to local brands, both in availability and in lower markups. Again, this discriminates not only against foreign suppliers, but also against suppliers from other provinces. In his speech on 17 June 1986, on the eve of the opening of bilateral negotiations in

Washington, Prime Minister Brian Mulroney tied the problems of interprovincial barriers to negotiations over international barriers:

Why can't you use Ontario bricks on a Quebec construction site? Why can't a Montrealer buy a bottle of beer brewed in the Maritimes when that same beer is a best seller in Washington, DC?[2]

Services

As economies have become more affluent, the relative importance of services has increased, compared to the production of goods.[3] Both North American nations have expressed an interest in considering freer international transactions in services. If significant bilateral progress can be made on trade in services, it may contribute to a broader multilateral negotiation on services in the current talks under the General Agreement on Tariffs and Trade. The United States is particularly interested in progress on services as a way of demonstrating to the rest of the world that agreements are possible in this area.[4] Services were covered in the US-Israel free trade agreement, but only in a general way: broad principles were set out, and both sides expressed their "desire to work toward international acceptance of these principles." The hope and expectation was that a more specific and binding agreement could be worked out later between Israel and the United States. The current US-Canadian negotiations represent another opportunity to become specific.

Services include, but are not limited to: travel and tourism; transportation; communications; insurance; banking services; other financial services; professional services, such as consulting in construction, engineering, accounting, and management; computer services; motion pictures; and advertising.

---

2. Barriers to interprovincial trade are described by Safarian (1980).
3. Regarding trade in services, see also Diebold and Stalson (1983); Hufbauer and Schott (1985, pp. 66–71); and Schott (1983).
4. In his congressional testimony of 1 October 1986, Harry L. Freeman, Executive Vice President, American Express, expresses a private-sector view that a US-Canadian agreement on services is desirable as "an example of what we want to achieve in the MTN" (Multilateral Trade Negotiations).

Travel and tourism is already quite free; a large number of tourists pass the border in both directions, with little inconvenience. Nevertheless, improvements might be made; one of the topics for negotiation, identified at the Shamrock Summit (March 1985), was an improved Air Transport Agreement, aimed at facilitating transborder travel. Furthermore, problems of advertising have arisen, such as the Canadian duties on promotional material for resort areas. Presumably, tariffs on such materials would be eliminated as part of a free trade agreement.

In the past year, Canada has been working on an overhaul of transportation policy, partly in response to deregulation in the United States, and partly, perhaps, as a background for bilateral negotiations. Canada's objective is to reduce regulation and encourage competition in all forms of transportation—air, trucking, railroads, and shipping. As transportation becomes more open and competitive domestically, it becomes easier to provide freer access to firms from the other country. Trucking is an area where the Canadian federal government has considerable leverage in determining national policy: it has jurisdiction over interprovincial transportation. (The Canadian government has delegated jurisdiction over interprovincial trucking to the provinces, but it retains constitutional rights in this area. Lipsey and Smith [1985, p. 142] suggest that the federal government can use this as a lever to enforce any agreement reached between Canada and the United States: if provinces fail to fall in line with an international agreement, the Canadian government could reclaim its authority over interprovincial trucking.)

Financial services are more complicated because the case for domestic regulation is much stronger than, say, in trucking or in manufacturing. The reason is twofold. First, it is very difficult for individuals to evaluate how well institutions are carrying out their fiduciary responsibilities. The typical consumer finds it much easier to judge the quality of a pair of shoes or a car than the quality of a life insurance policy. If my life insurance company will not pay off, I (or, rather, my family) will not find out until it is too late. Although some of the information problems can be eased by consumer information services (for example, those that compare premium charges on various types of life insurance policies), the question of whether institutions are meeting their fiduciary responsibilities can be addressed only by an agency with the authority to look at the insurance company or the bank's books. Second, banks have a particularly strategic role to play in the economy: their liabilities are the major component of the money stock, and runs on banks can create major macroeconomic disruptions. The sad experience of 1933 provided a compelling case for deposit insurance. If a government is going to guarantee bank liabilities, it had better look at the banks' books and have capital requirements for banks; otherwise, it may be signing a blank check to cover the costs of insider loans and financial buccaneering.

This does not mean that the more regulation, the better, and, of course, there has been substantial deregulation of financial institutions in recent years, particularly in the United States. There will, however, be a continuing question of the appropriate balance: what financial liabilities should be guaranteed, and what regulations should be imposed on institutions whose liabilities are guaranteed?

Internationally, free trade in financial services does not mean the absence of regulation; rather, it means that foreign financial institutions be provided national treatment: that is, they be permitted to carry on business on the same basis as domestic firms. In the US-Canadian case, there are two particular complications. First is the traditional US suspicion of large financial institutions, which can be traced back at least to the conflict between Andrew Jackson and the Second Bank of the United States, and which has led to the prohibition of interstate banking. It is true that this prohibition has been breaking down, in part as an ad hoc way of dealing with banks in trouble (by allowing them to be taken over by institutions in other states). Nevertheless, some restraints on interstate operations are likely to remain. This raises the question as to the appropriate access of Canadian banks to the US market. Clearly, if they were given unlimited access, this would not represent national treatment, but rather preferred treatment: They would have access not open to any US institution.

On the Canadian side, a major concern is the strategic role of financial institutions as lenders, and the influence they have in determining the flow of financial capital to other industries. If foreign institutions were to become major lenders in Canada, this might touch a sensitive political nerve; in particular, it might raise the concern in Canadian minds that foreign subsidiaries might have a preference over domestic firms in their access to financing.[5]

---

5. Many Americans, and some Canadians, are skeptical of this argument, noting that financial institutions are interested in making profits—that is, in maximizing their risk-

Nevertheless, the time does seem opportune to come to some agreement on financial services. Unlike the area of trade remedy laws, where the trend toward more formal procedures has made an agreement more difficult (while more desirable), the movement toward deregulation of financial institutions has facilitated the opening of markets to foreign competition. For example, recent steps by Ontario have included the relaxation of restrictions on foreign ownership of financial institutions. In the bilateral negotiations, one promising area for agreement is in computer services, including those for financial institutions, where R. Frazee of the Royal Bank of Canada has suggested a liberalization (1983).[6]

Regarding consulting services, two issues stand out—the quicker and easier cross-border passage of individuals who are going to do the consulting, and the establishment of branch offices in the other country. Branch offices raise not only questions of international investment, but also licensing. As licensing is often a state or provincial matter, with substantial barriers within each of the two nations, it is hard to envision a comprehensive international agreement that permits completely free access by the consultants of the partner nation. However, the "national treatment" of consultants from the other country might provide somewhat better access.

Investment

International investment, and the policies used to regulate such investment, have been a source of friction in US-Canadian relations.

For decades, many Canadians have been deeply concerned that foreign—and particularly US—ownership of their industry might lead to loss of control over their economic destiny. This concern has led the Canadian government to address two questions: How much foreign

---

adjusted returns in making loans. They operate as commercial institutions, not as the agents of the national interest. Nevertheless, the nationality of firms does sometimes seem to influence their behavior. For example, Japanese automobile manufactures use different production methods than US manufacturers, and National Westminster Bank USA has reportedly been more willing to make loans to small New York businesses than are the major New York banks.

6. Frazee (1983) and Rodney Grey (1983b). (Banking is one area where Canadian firms are larger than most US firms.)

investment should be permitted? And how can the Canadian government take steps to ensure that foreign subsidiaries will behave in the Canadian national interest? It was these two questions that led to the establishment of the Foreign Investment Review Agency (FIRA) in 1973, to screen foreign investment. Foreign firms could be denied permission to enter, and required to meet standards of performance as a condition of entry.

The first of these points is not the major bone of contention; the general right of countries to restrict inflows of investment is not contested. Furthermore, restriction of international investment is consistent with the establishment of a free trade agreement: such an agreement requires free movement of goods, but not the free movement of the factors of production (labor and capital). Nevertheless, the movement of capital in some cases is closely associated with the freer movement of goods and services. For example, if firms are going to have easy access to foreign markets, they must be allowed to set up marketing subsidiaries in foreign countries, and acquire warehouses and other marketing-support capital. (This is not a significant problem between the United States and Canada.) Similarly, relatively open access in the service sector may be difficult unless firms have the right to establish offices in the partner nations. This is a potential topic of negotiation as part of a possible US-Canadian agreement on services.

The major point of friction between the two governments has been the undertakings that investing firms negotiated with FIRA. (The law did not list specific performance requirements, but once an investing firm undertook specific commitments, they were legally binding.) Undertakings included export targets, and commitments that target amounts of Canadian parts and services would be used. Some firms undertook to replace specific dollar amounts of imports with Canadian made goods. Export requirements can have the effect of export subsidies or dumping, while the requirement for Canadian inputs can have the effect of nontariff barriers, by encouraging the substitution of Canadian products for items that would otherwise be imported. One Canadian rationale for these requirements was that US subsidiaries would automatically tend to buy parts from the United States unless they were required to explicitly consider Canadian suppliers—what might be called the affirmative action approach to procurement. (This approach was most clearly being taken when an investing firm undertook to set up a purchasing division in the Canadian subsidiary.) To the United States, the requirements represented protection. Furthermore, they represented protection that was difficult to identify and quantify, in part because the commitments of foreign investors were generally not made public. A GATT panel in 1983 found that the commitments to purchase Canadian inputs were contrary to GATT Article III, in that they afforded protection to domestic production.[7]

One objective of the Mulroney government has been to encourage foreign investment as a way of promoting growth. As part of the program of the new government, FIRA was replaced with a much less comprehensive and formal review procedure. (There will still be reviews of large acquisitions and foreign investment in culturally sensitive sectors.) This change has lowered the heat on the investment issue, although it is still too early to tell how the new Canadian investment policy will work in practice. Furthermore, a formal international agreement between the two countries should take into account not only present problems, but also what restrictions, if any, should be placed on a reinstitution of performance requirements like those of the FIRA.

One simple solution, along the lines of the US-Israeli free trade agreement and a recommendation by Lipsey and Smith (1985, p. 160) for a US-Canadian free trade association, would be to eliminate export and domestic content requirements as a condition for foreign investment. The two countries would each retain the right to decide whether or not to admit foreign investment, but, once admitted, the foreign firm would be provided national treatment—that is, it would have the same rights and responsibilities as domestically owned firms.[8]

This would be a good place to start in a search for a satisfactory solution to the foreign investment issue. In particular, Canada (and

---

7. However, the panel found that the export undertakings did not violate Article XVII.

For a discussion of performance requirements of Canada and other countries, see Safarian (1983) and Hufbauer and Shelton Erb (1984, pp. 81–83).

8. Article 13 of the US-Israeli agreement includes the commitment: "Neither Party shall impose, as a condition of establishment, expansion, or maintenance of investment by nationals or companies of the other Party, requirements to export . . . or to purchase locally produced goods and services." Lipsey and Smith (1985, p. 160), recommend that foreign subsidiaries not be subjected to "conditions with respect to employment, research and development, and exports that were not required of Canadian investors."

the United States) would undertake not to use investment requirements to suppress imports and promote exports—actions that can be considered inconsistent with a free trade arrangement. Two questions arise, however. The first is whether the commitment would apply only to subsidiaries of the partner nation, or to all investment, including investment by domestic firms (especially those that receive government grants for establishment or expansion) and investment from overseas countries. One difficulty is that Canadian performance requirements for subsidiaries of overseas firms (for example, the subsidiaries of Japanese auto firms) can provide incentives for exports from Canada to the United States. Thus, performance requirements are closely related to the export rebate issue considered in the previous chapter. In each case, the United States can be directly affected by arrangements between Canada and the subsidiaries of overseas firms.

The second question is whether Canada might use levers other than permission to invest as a way to impose domestic content requirements. On this point, neither Canadian history nor recent developments will be reassuring to Americans. Historically, Canadian content requirements have been a central feature of Canadian automotive policy; tariff rebates, rather than permission to invest, was the carrot. Nor were the amendments to the Patent Act proposed in mid-1986 reassuring. (These proposals have since been superseded.) Although the amendments would have dealt with one past source of friction—by providing a 10-year period of exclusive use, in contrast to the past compulsory licensing at low royalty rates—the amendments also contained a Canadian content provision. Specifically, to maintain exclusive use, a firm would have been required to begin manufacturing the active ingredient in Canada within a two-year period. (This requirement has been dropped in more recent proposals.)

Another important investment issue is what, if anything, can and should be done about bidding wars (offering tax concessions, etc.) to attract foreign plants. There is a common interest of bidders in limiting such bidding. But states and provinces are the principal bidders; it is not clear how they could be brought into an understanding between the two federal governments. One possibility would be to limit the total subsidies by all levels of government (federal, state or provincial, and local) as part of an agreement on the subsidy-countervailing duty issue (as suggested in the intermediate package in chapter 4). Governments would have an incentive to stay within the limit. If they did not, they would risk countervailing action.

Adjustment

While the GATT requires that a free trade agreement eliminate trade barriers on substantially all trade, barriers do not have to come down at once. An interim arrangement, with phased reduction of tariffs, is permissible, provided that barriers are eliminated and a free trade status achieved "within a reasonable length of time" (Article XXIV [5c]). An adjustment period lasting between 5 and 10 years is generally considered appropriate. The members of the European Community found the adjustment to lower tariffs was easier and less painful than expected; most of the adjustment was within industries rather than between industries. As a result, they accelerated their tariff-cutting schedule in 1960. This experience makes a case for leaning toward 5 years rather than 10. One advantage of a relatively brief period is that it may facilitate investment decisions: plants may be designed and built on the assumption that they will soon have duty-free access to the partner nation.

Two questions of timing have been raised for a prospective US-Canadian free trade agreement. One is whether the phased reduction of tariffs should be the same for both countries. Canadians frequently suggest that the Canadian phase-in period be longer than that of the United States, on the ground that the adjustment required of Canadian industry will be larger. For example, the Canadian phase-in period might be 10 years and the US period 5. There is, however, a major argument to be made against this proposal: the asymmetry of the automotive agreement has left a negative feeling in the United States; there is a substantial political advantage in keeping the terms of any new agreement as similar and equal as possible. (This does not mean that the agreement will work out equally in all respects. Canada will have the major adjustment problems. It will also be likely to reap the larger long-term gains, as explained in chapter 2.)

The second issue is whether the phase-in period should be the same for all industries. Adjustment does not necessarily take the same length of time in all sectors. An argument against differing phase-in periods is that they would complicate negotiations that are already difficult enough. However, this was not a major problem in the US-Israeli agreement, which provided for different phase-in periods for different products. Another option would be to have a uniform period, and leave open the possibility of an acceleration in some industries by mutual consent, once the transition has actually begun and more evidence on adjustment problems (or lack thereof) becomes available.

THE ROLE OF THE EXCHANGE RATE

Empirical work on US-Canadian free trade indicates that most of the adjustment would take place within industries, rather than between industries. For example, the Canadian chemical industry would not be run out of business by US competition; nor would the US industry have to retrench severely in the face of Canadian competition. Rather, producers on both sides of the border would tend to specialize in certain chemical products for domestic use and for export, and the imports of other chemicals would increase. This, of course, is one of the principal ways in which greater economies of scale can be achieved.

Nevertheless, the possibility that there will be a significant migration of industry from one country to the other must be addressed explicitly. What forces, if any, will prevent Canadian industry from outcompeting US industry over a wide range of goods, or US industry from driving much of Canadian industry out of business?

On this question, the exchange rate has a key role to play. Suppose, for example, that there were a broad and strong improvement in the Canadian competitive position compared to the United States as Canadian industry rationalized. As Canadian exports rose much more strongly than imports, the value of the Canadian dollar would tend to be bid up on foreign exchange markets, thereby raising the prices of Canadian imports in the United States. Similarly, a reduction in the value of the Canadian dollar would help to ensure that Canadian industry was not outcompeted all along the line.

The response of the exchange rate to changes in exports and imports is related closely to one of the advantages noted for freer trade in chapter 2—freer trade permits large-scale production to be combined with a high degree of competitiveness, even in a medium-sized country such as Canada. Domestic firms have relatively little market power because they must compete with imports. In addition, each domestic industry in one country (Canada, say) is competing with every other industry within the same country, via the exchange rate. If, for example, exports of a large set of Canadian industries rise strongly, this should strengthen the Canadian dollar, reducing the ability of other Canadian industries to export or to hold their domestic market in the face of cheaper imports.

Observe that, while the exchange rate provides a mechanism that can prevent a strong, general movement of production from one country to the other, it does not in itself prevent some industries from migrating from one country to the other, while other industries migrate in the opposite direction. Indeed, this possibility is foreseen in the standard textbook example where there are strong differences in comparative advantage. Why, then, do economists foresee most of the adjustment to a bilateral North American free trade agreement taking place within industries, rather than between them? The answer is that many differences in costs between the United States and Canada are attributable to the differing scale of production, not substantial differences in comparative advantage. With more open markets, much of the adjustment will occur in terms of specialization within industries. This is not, of course, to deny that some strong differences in comparative advantage do exist between the United States and Canada: for example, the United States has a clear and strong comparative advantage in the production of cotton, while Canada has a comparative advantage in nickel and newsprint. But trade is already free enough to have permitted specialization in such cases—Canada does not produce its own cotton, and the United States imports nickel and newsprint from Canada.

Although changes in the exchange rate can act as an important part of the adjustment process, they obviously do not keep imports and exports in lock step. Countries can and do run substantial imbalances in their international trade accounts. International capital flows, and current interest and dividend payments resulting from past capital flows, are two major reasons why.

If a country is a major importer of capital—as Canada has been for much of the past half century, and the United States has been for the past half decade—then the capital inflows will strengthen the currency and exert negative pressures on the trade balance. In this way, the exchange rate can also act as part of the adjustment process: when foreign nations provide us with financial capital (for example, by buying our bonds), our currency strengthens, and foreign nations also provide us with real capital (that is, they export more to us than we export to them). The combined financial capital and real resources can contribute to investment and the rate of growth in the recipient country, particularly if the economy is already operating at a high level of employment, and near capacity. Nevertheless, high capital inflows and a strong currency may be inappropriate; the resulting trade deficits may add to a high unemployment rate. A combination of large capital inflows and merchandise deficits is likely to cause heated policy debates—as it did in Canada in the late 1950s and early 1960s, and as it has been doing in the United States in recent years. The strongest conclusion from these two episodes is that it is important to get macroeconomic policies right—a point on which there have been major failings. In the early Canadian case, an overly tight monetary policy caused high interest rates and an excessive inflow of capital. In the recent US case, large government deficits have had the same effect.

This interrelationship between macroeconomic policies, exchange rates, and trade imbalances raises several major international policy issues. The first has to do with the possibility of macroeconomic policy coordination among nations. This topic has been addressed repeatedly at summit meetings and within the Organization for Economic Cooperation and Development. The actual coordination has been quite limited, for a very powerful reason: macroeconomic policy is generally aimed at difficult domestic problems, and may be subject to severe political constraints. For example, recommendations that the United States reduce its fiscal deficits, and thus reduce pressures on the international financial system, have repeatedly been made at summit meetings. There is a strong view in Congress and the administration that lower US budgetary deficits would be desirable. The difficulty is not to get agreement that US deficits are too high, but how to get a political agreement within the United States on the unpleasant spending cuts or tax increases needed to actually reduce them.

EXCHANGE RATE POLICY

The second major issue has to do with whether exchange rates should be managed actively by government jawboning, exchange market intervention, and changes in monetary and fiscal policies. Regarding intervention, there have been sharp swings in US policy—from moderate intervention during the Carter years, to a strict hands-off policy during the first Reagan administration, to the Plaza Agreement of the Group of Five (G-5) in September 1985 aimed at reducing exchange market misalignments. In the last half of 1985, intervention contributed to the decline in the value of the US dollar in terms of the DM, yen, and other currencies. But, while the Group of Five cooperated to bring down the dollar in the fall of 1985, not all has been harmonious. At the time of the IMF meetings in the fall of 1986, there was a clear difference of opinion between the United States and Germany. As a way of reducing the trade balance, the United States wanted a more expansive domestic aggregate demand policy in Germany, and a somewhat weaker dollar than did the Germans. More recently, in late 1986 and early 1987, European nations and Japan have intervened on the exchange market to moderate the slide of the dollar, while the US government has been reported to look favorably on some additional downward movement.

A STRONGER CANADIAN DOLLAR?

In past discussions of exchange rates in the United States, the focus has generally been on the yen and DM, with very little attention being paid to the Canadian dollar. This may seem odd, as Canada is the major trading and investment partner of the United States. Recently, however, a number of factors have attracted attention to the exchange value of the Canadian dollar. Most important has been the large US bilateral trade deficit with Canada ($17 billion in 1985, according to US statistics),[9] which has constituted a significant share of the overall US trade deficit ($124 billion in 1985, and even higher in 1986). In addition, the exchange value of the Canadian dollar has has been quite stable, at a time when the yen and the DM were appreciating strongly

---

9. According to Canadian statistics, the bilateral trade imbalance was only US$15 billion. Generally, Canadian statistics have shown Canada with a weaker bilateral trade picture than have US statistics. The discrepancy grew rapidly in the first half of 1986. At an annual rate, US statistics showed a bilateral trade deficit with Canada of US$19 billion, while Canadian statistics showed only US$12 billion. This statistical discrepancy is one reason why there can be a lack of agreement on the appropriate exchange rate.

against the US dollar. Since its low just below US70¢ in February 1986, the Canadian dollar has risen only modestly, to about 73.5¢ in mid-January 1987. The question accordingly has been raised: would a stronger Canadian dollar not help to reduce the US trade deficit?

This question is logically separable from commercial policy. Indeed, commercial policy changes—particularly major changes such as a free trade agreement that would be phased in over an extended period of 5 to 10 years—should be made with long-run equilibrium consequences in mind; they are not the way to deal with disequilibrium in the balance of payments. Nevertheless, it is when the Congress and administration have focused on the free trade issue that they have asked most pointedly: should the exchange value of the Canadian dollar not be increased, in order for Canada to "make a contribution" toward solving the US trade deficit?

From the Canadian side, several answers can be offered. First, Canada has already taken steps to strengthen its dollar. Because of an unwillingness to accept the inflationary consequences of a weaker currency, *the Bank of Canada has kept monetary policy tighter and interest rates higher than it otherwise would have done.* This policy has acted as a drag on the Canadian economy. Early in 1986 (and also on a number of other occasions), domestic interest rates were forced up to reverse a decline in the exchange value of the Canadian dollar. And Canadian authorities intervened in the exchange market, backing up their ability to do so with foreign bond flotations and drawings on standby lines of credit.

Second, while Canada has a trade surplus with the United States, it also has a substantial bilateral deficit on services. As a result, the bilateral current account imbalance is much less than the bilateral trade imbalance. According to US statistics, the bilateral current account deficit with Canada was less than $9 billion in 1985, compared to a trade deficit of $17 billion.

Third, Canada's overall payments position—with all other countries as a group—is not strong. It is true that Canada ran annual current account surpluses of about C$3 billion (as measured in Canadian statistics) between 1982 and 1984, but its current account swung back into deficit in 1985 and 1986. Furthermore, if Canada were to include its large negative net retained earnings in its current account—and thus follow the statistical definitions of the United States and the

International Monetary Fund—then the 1982-84 surpluses would disappear, and the expected 1986 current account deficit would exceed C$10 billion. As a percentage of GNP (somewhat more than 2 percent), this is approaching the comparable US current account deficit (over 3 percent of GNP). In short, Canada does not have a strong current account position; indeed, its position is almost as weak as that of the United States. It has not gained a strong payments position at the expense of the United States. Its bilateral trade surplus with the United States is a reflection of several factors—negative net interest and earnings, which weaken the current account and require a compensating overall trade surplus (at least in the long run); and the underlying disequilibrium between the United States and the rest of the world, with Canada being caught in the middle.

Nevertheless, the exchange value of the Canadian dollar may appropriately be considered in international discussions, particularly now that Canada and Italy have asked that the G-5 be expanded into a Group of Seven (G-7). In present circumstances, Canada would not necessarily oppose a *slightly* higher value for its dollar—perhaps 1¢ or so. In an appendix to this study, John Williamson estimates that the equilibrium value of the Canadian dollar is about US74¢, or slightly higher than the current price. This low estimate may seem surprising; there is a common view that the depreciation of the Canadian dollar since 1980 has given Canada a strong competitive advantage. However, changes in the exchange rate have been approximately offset by differences in domestic inflation and productivity. The Bank of Canada estimates that the unit labor cost in Canadian manufacturing, relative to that in the United States, is within 1 percent of where it was in 1980, after adjustment is made for changes in the exchange rate.

If the United States wants a higher Canadian dollar so that Canada can "make a contribution" to a reduction of the US trade deficit, perhaps Canada in return might expect the United States to make a contribution to moving the exchange rate. As Canada has already tightened its monetary policy and intervened in exchange markets to strengthen the Canadian dollar, perhaps the United States could be the country to put additional upward pressure on the Canadian dollar by engaging in official purchases of the Canadian dollar in exchange markets. A higher Canadian dollar brought on in this way would ease the dilemma facing Canadian macroeconomic policymakers; they would be free to have a somewhat more expansive monetary policy, while still meeting the exchange rate target. The resulting stimulus to the Canadian economy would also contribute (modestly) to US exports. In short, moderate US steps to strengthen the Canadian dollar, combined with a somewhat more expansive Canadian monetary policy, might contribute to the policy objectives of both countries.

FREE TRADE AND CHANGES IN EXCHANGE RATES

The above discussion has been based on the current balance of payments situation and outlook, and the tacit assumption that current commercial policies will be continued. In the event of a free trade agreement between the two countries, what would be the implications for the exchange rate?

Free trade would have a much more profound effect on the Canadian than on the US economy. Canadian real incomes—including real wages—would increase as Canadian industry reorganized and became more efficient. The Canadian gains could be taken in either—or a combination—of two forms:

● *higher nominal wages*

● *lower domestic prices,* and a *stronger Canadian dollar,* than would occur in the absence of a free trade agreement.

The choice between the two depends on macroeconomic policies yet to be determined. But the most likely outcome would be some strengthening of the Canadian dollar. (Again, this is compared to where it would go in the absence of a free trade agreement. Over the past decade, Canada has had more inflation, and a weakening dollar; a positive response does not mean that the exchange rate of the Canadian dollar would rise in the future. It might just fall more slowly than it otherwise would.)

In spite of such exchange rate consequences, it is not desirable to make exchange rates an integral part of the current free trade negoti- ations; they are already complicated enough. There is no compelling reason to depart from the traditional separation of trade negotiations (through the GATT and bilateral talks) and exchange rate matters (through the International Monetary Fund and such groups as the G-5 and G-7). Particularly now that Canada is part of the expanded G-7, that is the appropriate forum for exchange rate matters. In the event of free trade, it would be appropriate for the United States to push for a higher Canadian dollar under some circumstances—most notably, if the United States had a large current account deficit, while Canada had a sizable current account surplus and rising foreign exchange reserves. Put another way: if free trade resulted in a sizable swing of the Canadian current account into surplus, it would be desirable for the Canadian government to allow a rise in the exchange value of their dollar, and not oppose such a rise by rapid reserve accumulations. In this way, the exchange rate could contribute to the overall adjustment process.

Rules of Origin

Even within a free trade association, border controls are necessary, both to enforce immigration laws and to attempt to stop the passage of prohibited items such as firearms and drugs. In addition, customs houses are necessary to deal with excepted items (such as some agricultural products) that are still subject to tariffs or other barriers, and with transshipments from third countries.

Within a free trade association, each country undertakes to provide duty-free admission to (most) goods produced in the other member countries. But, unlike the case of a customs union, each country retains its separate tariff schedules on imports from outside nations. (For this reason, Canada would be unwilling to consider a customs union—most of the decisions on the common tariff would be made in Washington, with Canada losing control over its own commercial policy. The United States has no dispute with Canada on this point; it does not wish to impose its schedule of duties on Canada.)

The maintenance of separate tariffs means that, in the absence of customs regulations at the border, there would be an incentive to ship overseas goods through the lower tariff country, into the higher tariff partner. For example, with the United States having lower tariffs than Canada on automobiles, there would be an incentive for German auto makers to ship cars to the United States, pay the lower tariff, and then send them on to Canada. To prevent such roundabout evasion of tariffs, it is standard procedure to have *rules of origin* within a free trade association: goods may pass duty free only if a certain percentage of their value (for example, 50 percent) has been added within the nations of the free trade association.[10] Otherwise, they are not covered by the free trade agreement and are subject to the regular tariff of the importing nation as they pass the border.

THE DRAWBACK PROBLEM

While rules of origin deal with the most obvious problem of products from third countries, a technical difficulty remains, having to do with tariff drawbacks. It is standard procedure for firms to receive drawbacks of duties paid on imported products when those products are reexported, either in the form in which they were imported, or as components of a larger product. (The US duty drawback provision was established in 1789.) Such drawbacks are quite different from the duty remissions discussed in the last chapter. Unlike those duty remissions, drawbacks do not represent an indirect subsidy; rather, they are the return of a duty already paid on the item exported. (This distinction may be seen by considering an example: an auto part produced entirely in Canada, with 100 percent domestic content. It would not qualify for any drawback, since it would have no imported components, and therefore no duties would have been paid. However, its export would earn an overseas firm a rebate of duties on other imports into Canada, under the rebate program discussed in the last chapter.) So long as drawbacks do not exceed the amount of the duty actually levied on the imported product which is being reexported, they are explicitly permitted by the GATT (Article VI paragraph 4).

In an MFN world, with no free trade groupings, this drawback provision raises no major difficulties.[11] Drawbacks are provided for

---

10. The Auto Pact of 1965 (annex B) permitted duty-free entry of autos and original equipment parts from Canada only if they contained 50 percent North American value added.

11. For problems arising when drawbacks exceed the initial duty (and thus become subsidies), or when like inputs are substituted for the ones actually imported, see Hufbauer and Shelton Erb (1984, pp. 65–66).

reexports; tariffs are imposed by the countries into which the goods are being imported.

Within a free trade association, however, drawbacks might cause distortions and excessive shipments among members. To see why, consider an illustration, where both the United States and Canada manufacture a product. Assume that production costs are the same in the two countries; in making the product, each country adds $60 of value, and uses $40-worth of parts (exclusive of duties) imported from overseas. Suppose that the US duty on imported parts is 10 percent (that is, $4), and the Canadian duty 15 percent (that is, $6). The home-produced good sells for $104 in the United States and $106 in Canada; that is, domestic value added plus the cost of imported parts.

If a free trade association requires (say) 50 percent North American value added, this item qualifies for duty-free passage between the United States and Canada. Suppose that drawbacks are granted on Canadian exports to the United States. Then the Canadian product can be sold in the United States at $100 (that is, $106 less the $6 drawback of duties paid on parts imported from overseas), or for less than the US product ($104). Similarly, the US good can be sold in Canada for $100 (that is, $104 less a $4 drawback), or for less than the domestically produced good ($106). There will be uneconomic cross-shipment; there will be a tendency for each country to sell in the other nation.

On the other hand, if no duty drawback is permitted on shipments between the association members, then producers would be at a disadvantage in the country with the higher duty on imports. In the above example, Canadian producers would have costs of $106 (that is, $2 more than US producers), and they would have difficulty selling in the United States, even though they were just as efficient as US producers.

DEALING WITH THE DRAWBACK PROBLEM

There are several ways to deal with the drawback issue:

● Prohibit drawbacks on trade *within* the free trade association. This would eliminate the incentive to cross-ship between the members. But it would leave an advantage to the country with the lower duties on inputs imported from outside the free trade association. (Consequently, this first choice would create an incentive for member countries to lower their duties on inputs from third countries. That is, it would be consistent with a broad move toward freer trade with outside countries, and would reduce the amount of trade diversion.)

• Permit drawbacks, but only on the amount by which the tariff on inputs exceeds the corresponding tariff in the partner nation. In the above example, Canadian firms would be given a drawback of only $2; that is, the $6 of Canadian tariff less the $4 US tariff on similar overseas imports or inputs.

• Permit drawbacks, but allow the importing country to then impose its tariff on the inputs imported from nonmember countries. In the example, Canada would grant a drawback of $6, while the US would impose a tariff of $4 on the item because of its third-country content. This third option would be equivalent to the second, except for the transfer from the treasury of the exporting nation to the treasury of the importing nation, and the administrative complications.

In addition to being complicated, the third option has the disadvantage that it might seem to be a departure from free bilateral trade— for example, tariffs would be imposed by the United States on goods coming from Canada. It might be difficult for people to understand that there really is a free trade association if tariffs were collected on many products as they passed the border (even though the tariffs were not on Canadian value added, but only on the overseas imports used in the Canadian product).

I would favor the first option, even though it is imperfect. One advantage is that it could be put into a simple package, along with duty rebates: no drawbacks or tariff rebates would be given for exports to the partner nation. This is the general[12] rule within the European Free Trade Association. (Because a common market has a common tariff on imports from outside countries, no problem is raised by this first option, and it is the one used within the European Community.)

---

12. Complications include an exception for duties paid on imports from other members (as occurs during the transition to zero tariffs). EFTA 1982, annex B, Article 23.

6   Summary and Conclusions

Bilateral free trade would contribute to the efficiency of the North American economies, and to their competitiveness in facing overseas producers. Access to a larger market would be beneficial to both countries, and particularly Canada; it would allow producers to specialize and gain the advantages of large-scale production. Much of the specialization would take place within industries, and even within plants. Empirical work taking economies of scale into account suggests that the gains from bilateral free trade would be large; Harris and Cox estimate 9 percent of Canadian GNP (chapter 2). The importance of economies of scale shows up in the contrast between the Harris-Cox results and those of economists who worked with models in which constant returns to scale were assumed. In those constant-returns studies, the gains either disappeared or were quite small (less than 1 percent of GNP).

For the United States, much less is at stake than for Canada—both in absolute terms, and, *a fortiori,* as a percentage of the much larger US GNP. Because the reorganization of US industry would be so much less pronounced, US industry runs much smaller risks; but the United States also has less to gain. Because free trade would increase the size of the market to which US industry has open access by about 7 percent, it would provide scope for longer production runs for US businesses, particularly those close to the Canadian border with relatively quick and easy access. The larger market would also have two related advantages—it would ease the antitrust problem, making it more possible to have the advantages both of larger firms and more competitive market conditions. And the larger North American "home" base would improve the ability of firms, both US and Canadian, to export into the increasingly competitive world market and to meet the competition of imports from overseas.

139

Problem Areas

Chapters 4 and 5 deal with some of the problems facing the trade negotiators. One of the most complex has to do with the countervailing duty (CVD) law and other "trade remedy laws," which are commonly known in Canada as "contingent protection." This difference in terminology is not a trivial matter; it reflects a fundamental difference in attitudes. In the United States, the CVD law is not considered *protection*, but rather a *remedy* for distortions previously introduced into the system. Protection interferes with the operation of market-driven comparative advantage. But government subsidies also distort the signals of the market; they can give foreign exporters an artificial—and unfair—advantage. What a CVD does is to offset this unfair advantage, and allow trading patterns to correspond more closely to underlying market forces. According to this view, CVD is the opposite of protection; it does not create, but rather reduces distortions. To some of the stronger proponents of the CVD law, the fact that the United States also has a list of subsidies that can benefit exports is no defense of Canadian subsidies; if Canada wants to impose CVD in such cases to offset the effects of the subsidies, that will improve international efficiency, too. A further argument for the CVD law is the deterrent effect it can exert: it discourages countries from introducing trade-distorting subsidies in the first place.

The Canadian view—as expressed by Rodney Grey and others—is that US trade remedy laws are a way of keeping up trade barriers in the face of the cuts in tariffs negotiated in the various rounds under the General Agreement on Tariffs and Trade (GATT). Duties are duties—whether they come from the standard tariff, or are special duties under escape clauses, countervail, and so forth. The purpose is to protect domestic producers from foreign competition. Furthermore, because "contingent protection" is unpredictable, it is exceptionally troublesome for a country that has a limited domestic market and needs access to large foreign markets to gain economies of scale. Canadians are particularly concerned by the tendency of the United States to define countervailable subsidies more and more broadly. *Assured, predictable* access to the US market is one of the major Canadian objectives in the current negotiations.

Chapter 4 provides details on two important cases which illustrate how complex the subsidy and CVD issue is: the auto industry (which accounts for about one-third of total trade between the two countries), and softwood lumber (where Canadian exports of US$3 billion constitute about 4 percent of total Canadian exports to the United States).

In the auto case, the Canadian rebate scheme has led to recent objections from the United States. Duty rebates on cars can be earned by exports of quite different products (for example, automotive parts); they constitute an export subsidy. Furthermore, regardless of how puzzling and ill-defined some aspects of US CVD policy may be, there would seem to be little reason for Canadians to be surprised by US objections to the rebate scheme; the US reaction may be unwelcome, but it should scarcely be unpredictable. A US court suit over auto rebates led to the establishment of the Auto Pact two decades ago, and the United States objected to a very similar rebate scheme for Volkswagen in the late 1970s. Unless Canada eliminates the auto rebates, they are likely to put stress on the bilateral relationship in general, and the Auto Pact in particular—whether the free trade talks are pursued or not.

The chance of trouble in the automotive industry is increased by the disproportionate share of East Asian manufacturing being established in Canada. On Canadian automobile rebates, my conclusions are straightforward. They should be eliminated. They are a violation of the GATT subsidies code. They are a type of subsidy to which the United States has repeatedly objected in the past. They are politically dangerous, particularly because they permit firms to earn duty-free imports from Japan by exporting to the United States. They represent a time bomb in US-Canadian relations: the explosion is most likely to occur several years down the road, after substantial East Asian investment is already in place in Canada, and when Canadian exports from these plants are rising.

The timber stumpage issue is much less clear. Here, it should be easy to understand why Canadians complain about the use of the CVD law to harass their exporters, and over unpredictable extensions of the US law—particularly in the light of the earlier US decision in 1983, that Canadian stumpage practices did not represent a countervailable subsidy. The merits of the case are murky. It is possible for British Columbia to use its system to subsidize exports, but the system is not, on the face of it, unreasonable. One conclusion does stand out: it is not appropriate to consider any discrepancy between US and foreign resource prices as a subsidy *ipso facto*. A Canadian comparative advantage is one of the basic forces in operation in softwood lumber. Indeed, it is the size of the available lumber cut in Canada, not the existence of a subsidy, which constitutes the main threat to the US industry. Perhaps in such cases the United States should consider shifting the focus of policy from CVD to escape clause actions. Perhaps the issue should not be whether a Canadian subsidy can be detected, but whether the disruptions to the US industry justify temporary barriers to imports. Because of its complexity, stumpage is the type of issue where a joint US-Canadian disputes commission might play a useful role.

Because of the sharply different viewpoints in the two countries, the subsidy and CVD issue is one of the most difficult in the current negotiations. At the end of chapter 4, several possible negotiating packages were presented. The least ambitious would include a Canadian elimination of auto duty rebates; an increase in the *de minimis* provision, so that no CVD would be imposed for subsidies less than 2 percent or 2.5 percent; and an agreement to refer new trade remedy cases to an international commission at an early stage. An intermediate package would include the above items, plus: an agreement to exempt each other from future extensions of trade remedy laws; some agreement defining acceptable, unacceptable, and "gray" practices more clearly; an agreement to limit gray area subsidies to no more than, say, 4 percent or 5 percent of the value of the product; and a further increase in the threshold level—below which CVD would not be imposed—to the same 4 percent or 5 percent. If both sides kept the agreement, eliminating unacceptable practices and holding "gray" subsidies below the threshold, countervailing duties would not in practice be applied to the exports of the other country. However, each country would retain a unilateral right to impose them if the other country violated the established guidelines (the elimination of unacceptable practices, and the limiting of "gray" subsidies).

A more ambitious approach would be similar to that in the European Community, where the EC Commission reviews subsidy practices, and whose decisions can lead to legal action in the European Court of Justice.

Chapter 5 considers the coverage of a free trade agreement, and nontariff topics such as government procurement. Regarding coverage, agriculture is a problem because of the extent of government support programs. It would not seem feasible to include all agricultural products in a free trade agreement, although some products could be included. Outside agriculture, the wider the coverage the better. Once exceptions for industrial products are considered, there is a danger that the negotiations might unravel. Furthermore, it is desirable to make an agreement broad enough to meet GATT Article XXIV; there is a compelling economic rationale for that article.

In the preceding two chapters, the focus has been on the problems and sources of friction between the two countries. This has been quite intentional—after all, negotiations are largely aimed at dealing with disagreements. But this focus also has a danger, that we may become so preoccupied with the trees that we miss the forest. The trees are the multitude of frictions on specific policies. The forest is the strong mutual interest in an open trading relationship, which can contribute to an efficient North American economy.

A Possible Agreement in 1987?

Now that negotiations are under way, success may depend on keeping up momentum. September 1987 is an important target date. An agreement by that time would give the required period for congressional consideration, prior to the expiration of the fast track authority in early 1988. Although a reauthorization of the fast track may be included in 1987 trade legislation, there are other reasons to aim for a 1987 agreement. By 1988, US distractions will include the presidential election. Prime Minister Brian Mulroney will also be facing an election in 1988 or 1989. If the current window of opportunity is missed, it may not soon recur. The free trade issue will not die; trade between the two countries is too important. At some time in the future, bilateral free trade will once again be seriously considered. But the issue can go into hibernation. As has happened in the past, a failure to agree on freer trade may cause the pendulum to swing in the opposite direction, toward a more nationalist economic policy in Canada.

An agreement might include the following important components:

1. *Elimination of Tariffs on All Nonagricultural, and Some Agricultural Products*. To ease the adjustment, a phase-in period of 5 to 10 years

is appropriate. For reasons explained toward the end of chapter 5, a bilateral zero-tariff regime would require changes in the drawback law. An appropriate approach would be to phase out drawbacks on bilateral trade in the same period of 5 to 10 years.

2. *A Narrowing of Differences on Trade Remedy Laws.* One Canadian hope, in entering the negotiations, was to achieve exemption from US trade remedy laws, particularly the CVD law. In the present situation, with large US trade deficits and strong congressional support for a tightening of the CVD law, such a blanket exemption does not seem possible. Furthermore, it is not clear that Canada would be willing to eliminate its own "contingent protection," particularly antidumping duties. Although the gains and risks of any agreement are asymmetric—with Canada facing both the greater risks and the greater gains—it is important to keep the agreement itself symmetrical; it would be out of the question to eliminate US "contingent protection" but not Canadian.

Although a comprehensive agreement on exemptions from trade protection laws does not seem possible, differences might be narrowed. It should be possible to reach agreement on the unambitious package listed earlier: an increase in the *de minimis* to 2 percent or 2.5 percent, the elimination of the Canadian auto duty rebates, and the agreement to refer trade remedy cases to a bilateral commission. I would hope that it might be possible to go farther, to the intermediate package: an agreement on unacceptable and "gray" area subsidies, an agreement to limit "gray" subsidies to 4 percent or 5 percent, and an increase in the threshold to the same 4 percent or 5 percent. With such a package, the CVD-subsidy issue should no longer be a major bone of contention between the two nations.

If this intermediate package proves unachievable in 1987, a two-stage strategy might be adopted. The initial 1987 agreement would include the unambitious package. But there would also be an undertaking to work toward a second, more ambitious agreement in the future.

3. *Government Procurement.* At the federal level, firms from the partner country might be given equal access to procurement. Provincial and state procurement practices will be tougher to deal with. However, an agreement might cover certain aspects of provincial and state practices—for example, alcoholic beverage marketing.

4. *Investment Incentives and Related National Preferences.* "Buy American" or "Buy Canadian" provisions can occur not only in government procurement; they have also occurred in the performance requirements of the old Canadian Foreign Investment Review Agency (FIRA). These included requirements to buy Canadian goods (which could act as a barrier to imports) and export requirements (which could have an effect similar to an export subsidy). Although FIRA has been replaced by a much less comprehensive review process, agreements should be made for the long run; the United States is interested in a Canadian commitment not to use the investment lever to limit US access to the Canadian market, or to stimulate exports in an uneconomic manner. An agreement might also rule out the use of other "levers" to encourage or require domestic production, such as the requirement in the now superseded pharmaceutical proposals, which would have required the Canadian manufacture of active ingredients by drug companies. Commitments not to impose such domestic preferences might go hand-in-hand with an agreement on government procurement.

5. *Services.* An agreement could include at least a statement of general principles for liberalization of services, similar to that of the US-Israeli agreement. It might be possible to go further, and include specific coverage in some areas. Financial services and transportation are two possibilities. Financial services raise a complication, because they are one area where the case for domestic regulation is particularly strong—namely, regulation of fiduciary responsibilities. National treatment might be a target to aim for. Ontario is currently taking steps to provide freer access to foreign financial institutions. The possibilities of freer trade in transportation services will depend in part on Canadian deregulation legislation, currently under consideration. Access to the other country's highways can make a significant contribution to the international flow of goods.

6. *Bilateral Commission.* A permanent bilateral commission should be established to deal with trade disputes. Although it seems unlikely that the two countries will be willing to grant such a commission the powers of the EC Commission to enforce its decisions, it could perform a useful advisory function. Provisions might be made to refer trade disputes to the commission at an early stage. For example, subsidy complaints could be submitted to the bilateral commission

before the US International Trade Commission and the Commerce Department issue their findings.

While the United States is particularly interested in the fourth point, Canada has a special interest in points two and six. A broad agreement, where the principal concerns of each country are addressed, might have a better chance of acceptance by Congress and by provinces than would a narrow agreement on just one or two items.

Such an agreement would leave loose ends, which could be the subjects of future negotiations—for example, unfinished business on procurement by state and provincial governments. But it would be an historic step.

This is not to suggest that an agreement will be easy; there are formidable political barriers in its way. In the United States, one problem is how to get trade with Canada moved up on the agenda, so that, even briefly, it makes it into the top 25 items in the list of priorities. Only then may it be possible to concentrate on some of the compromises necessary to smooth the way to an agreement. In Canada, the problem is the opposite—how to get trade negotiations demoted from the front page to the business section. Otherwise it may not be possible to take the political heat generated by the compromise process. The *Financial Post* (Toronto) has neatly identified the problem for negotiators (19 January 1987, p. 3). They are "seemingly trapped between Canadian free-trade touchiness and American indifference." Neither side will get an ideal agreement. But it should be possible to get an agreement that will contribute to the efficiency of the North American economy, to the benefit of both parties.

References

American Textile Manufacturers Institute, Inc. 1986. *Statement filed with the US International Trade Commission.* 19 September. Processed.

Anjaria, Shailendra J., Naheed Kirmani, and Arne B. Petersen. 1985. *Trade Policy Issues and Developments.* Washington: International Monetary Fund.

Baldwin, John R., and Paul K. Gorecki. 1983a. "Trade, Tariffs and Relative Plant Scale in Canadian Manufacturing Industries: 1970–1979." Discussion Paper 232. Ottawa: Economic Council of Canada.

——. 1983b. "The Relationship Between Plant Scale and Product Diversity in Canadian Manufacturing Industries." Discussion Paper 237. Ottawa: Economic Council of Canada.

——. 1983c. "Trade, Tariffs, Product Diversity and Length of Production Run in Canadian Manufacturing Industries: 1970–1979." Discussion Paper 247. Ottawa: Economic Council of Canada.

——. 1986. *The Role of Scale in Canada-US Productivity Differences in the Manufacturing Sector.* Toronto: University of Toronto Press in cooperation with the Royal Commission on the Economic Union and Development Prospects for Canada.

Beigie, Carl E. 1970. *The Canada-US Automotive Trade Agreement: An Evaluation.* Washington: National Planning Association.

Boadway, Robin, and John Treddenick. 1978. "A General Equilibrium Computation of the Effects of the Canadian Tariff Structure." *Canadian Journal of Economics,* vol. 11, no.3 (August), pp. 424–46.

Bond, David, and Ronald J. Wonnacott. 1968. *Trade Liberalization and the Canadian Furniture Industry.* Toronto: University of Toronto Press for the Private Planning Association of Canada.

Brown, Drusilla K., and Robert M. Stern. 1987. "Evaluating the Effects of US-Canadian Free Trade: What Do the Multisector Trade Models Suggest?" In Stern, Trezise, and Whalley, forthcoming.

Carmichael, Edward A. 1985. *Reorienting the Canadian Economy: Policy Review and Outlook, 1986.* Toronto: C.D. Howe Institute.

Cline, William R., ed. 1983. *Trade Policies in the 1980s.* Washington: Institute for International Economics.

Cline, William R. 1982. *"Reciprocity": A New Approach to World Trade Policy?* POLICY ANALYSES IN INTERNATIONAL ECONOMICS 2. Washington: Institute for International Economics, September.

Colombo, John Robert. 1974. *Colombo's Canadian Quotations.* Edmonton: Hurtig Publishers.

147

Cox, David, and Richard G. Harris. 1985. "Trade Liberalization and Industrial Organization: Some Estimates for Canada." *Journal of Political Economy,* vol. 93, no. 1 (February), pp. 115–45.

Crandall, Robert W. 1987. "The US and Canadian Steel Industries." In Stern, Trezise, and Whalley, forthcoming.

Deardorff, Alan V., and Robert M. Stern. 1983. "The Economic Effects of Complete Elimination of Post-Tokyo Round Tariffs." In Cline, ed.

Department of External Affairs. 1983. *Canadian Trade Policy for the 1980s.* Ottawa.

———. 1985. *Canadian Trade Negotiations: Introduction, Selected Documents, Further Reading.* Ottawa.

Diebold, William, Jr., and Helena Stalson. 1983. "Negotiating Issues in International Services Transactions." In Cline, ed.

Eastman, Harry, and Stefan Stykolt. 1967. *The Tariff and Competition in Canada.* Toronto: Macmillan.

Economic Council of Canada. 1986. *Changing Times.* Twenty-Third Annual Review. Ottawa.

English, H. Edward. 1964. *Industrial Structure in Canada's International Competitive Position.* Montreal: Private Planning Association of Canada.

European Free Trade Association. 1982. *Convention Establishing the European Free Trade Association* (as amended). Geneva.

Feller, Peter B. 1969. "Mutiny Against the Bounty: An Examination of Subsidies, Border Tax Adjustments, and the Resurgence of the Countervailing Duty Law." *Law and Policy in International Business,* vol. 1, pp. 17–76.

Frazee, R. 1983. *Trade and Technology: It's Canada's Move.* Montreal: Royal Bank of Canada.

Freeman, Harry L. 1986. "The Case for a US-Canada Free-Trade Agreement." Testimony Before the Economic Stabilization Subcommittee, House Banking Committee, US Congress. 1 October. Processed.

General Agreement on Tariffs and Trade. 1983. *Canada: Administration of the Foreign Investment Review Act.* L/5504. Geneva, 25 July.

Granatstein, J.L. 1985. "Free Trade Between Canada and the United States: The Issue That Will Not Go Away." In *The Politics of Canada's Economic Relationship with the United States.* Edited by Denis Stairs and Gilbert R. Winham. Toronto: University of Toronto Press in cooperation with the Royal Commission on the Economic Union and Development Prospects for Canada.

Grey, Rodney de C. 1982. *United States Trade Policy Legislation: A Canadian View.* Montreal: Institute for Research on Public Policy.

———. 1983a. "A Note on US Trade Practices." In Cline, ed.

———. 1983b. *Traded Computer Services: An Analysis of a Proposal for Canada/USA Agreement.* Montreal: Royal Bank of Canada.

———. 1984. "Some Notes on Subsidies and the International Rules." In *Interface Three: Legal Treatment of Domestic Subsidies.* Edited by Don Wallace, Jr., Frank J. Loftus, and Van Z. Krikorian. Washington: International Law Institute.

Hamilton, Bob, and John Whalley. 1985. "Geographically Discriminatory Trade Arrangements." *Review of Economics and Statistics,* vol. 67, no. 3 (August), pp. 446–55.

Harris, Richard G. 1984. "Applied General Equilibrium Analysis of Small Open

Economies and Imperfect Competition." *American Economic Review,* vol. 74, no. 5 (December), pp. 1016–32.

———. 1985. "Summary of a Project on the General Equilibrium Evaluation of Canadian Trade Policy," in Whalley and Hill (1985), p. 157–77.

Harris, Richard G., with David Cox. 1984. *Trade, Industrial Policy and Canadian Manufacturing.* Toronto: Ontario Economic Council.

Hill, Roderick, and John Whalley. 1985. "Canada-US Free Trade: An Introduction." In Whalley and Hill (1985).

Hufbauer, Gary Clyde, and Howard F. Rosen. 1986. *Domestic Adjustment and International Trade.* POLICY ANALYSES IN INTERNATIONAL ECONOMICS 15. Washington: Institute for International Economics, March.

Hufbauer, Gary C., and Andrew J. Samet. 1985. "United States Response to Canadian Initiatives for Sectoral Trade Liberalization: 1983–84." In *The Politics of Canada's Economic Relationship with the United States.* Edited by Denis Stairs and Gilbert R. Winham. Toronto: University of Toronto Press in cooperation with the Royal Commission on the Economic Union and Development Prospects for Canada.

Hufbauer, Gary Clyde, and Jeffrey J. Schott. 1985. *Trading for Growth: The Next Round of Trade Negotiations.* POLICY ANALYSES IN INTERNATIONAL ECONOMICS 11. Washington: Institute for International Economics, September.

Hufbauer, Gary Clyde, and Joanna Shelton Erb. 1984. *Subsidies in International Trade.* Washington: Institute for International Economics.

Johnson, Harry G. 1963. "The Bladen Plan for Increased Protection of the Canadian Automobile Sector." *Canadian Journal of Economics and Political Science,* vol. 29, no. 2 (May), pp. 212–38.

Kelleher, James F. 1985. Report to Prime Minister Mulroney (The "Kelleher Report"). 17 September, reprinted in Department of External Affairs, 1985.

Lea, Sperry. 1987. "What a Difference Twenty-One Years Make: A Possible Plan for a Canada-US Free Trade Area." In Stern, Trezise, and Whalley, forthcoming.

Lipsey, Richard G. 1957. "The Theory of Customs Unions: Trade Diversion and Welfare." *Economica,* vol. 24, no. 93 (February), pp. 40–46.

Lipsey, Richard G, and Murray G. Smith. 1985. *Taking the Initiative: Canada's Trade Options.* Toronto: C.D. Howe Institute.

Longworth, David. 1985. "Some Exchange Rate Policy Considerations When Trade Is Liberalized." In *Domestic Policies and the International Economic Environment.* Edited by John Whalley. Toronto: University of Toronto Press in cooperation with the Royal Commission on the Economic Union and Development Prospects for Canada.

Magun, Sunder. 1986. "The Effects of Canada-US Free Trade on the Canadian Labour Market. Paper presented at the meetings of the Canadian Economics Association. Winnipeg, 29 May. Processed.

Meade, James E. 1955. *The Theory of Customs Unions.* Amsterdam: North Holland.

Morici, Peter. 1987. "An American View of the US-Canada Free Trade Negotiations." Washington: National Planning Association. Paper presented at Brookings Institution Conference on US-Canadian Free Trade, 3 February.

Moroz, Andrew R. 1985. "Canada-US Automotive Trade and Trade Policy Issues." In Ontario Economic Council, *Canada-US Trade and Investment Issues.* Toronto.

Moroz, Andrew R., and Gregory J. Meredith. 1985. *Economic Effects of Trade*

Liberalization with the USA: Evidence and Questions. Discussion Paper 8510. Ottawa: Institute for Research on Public Policy.

Mulroney, Brian. 1985. Statement to the House of Commons, 26 September, reprinted in Department of External Affairs, 1985.

Reisman, Simon S. 1984. "The Issue of Free Trade." In *US-Canadian Economic Relations: Next Steps?* Edited by Edward R. Fried and Philip H. Trezise. Washington: Brookings.

Royal Commission on the Automobile Industry (the Bladen Commission). 1962. *Report.* Ottawa.

Royal Commission on the Economic Union and Development Prospects for Canada (the Macdonald Commission). 1985. *Report,* vol. 1. Ottawa.

Rugman, Alan M., and Andrew Anderson. 1987. "Administered Protection: American 'Unfair Trade' Law as a Non-tariff Barrier to Trade." *World Economy,* vol. 10, no. 1 (March).

Safarian, A.E. 1966. *Foreign Ownership of Canadian Industry.* Toronto: McGraw-Hill.

————. 1980. "Ten Markets or One? Regional Barriers to Economic Activity in Canada." Toronto: Ontario Economic Council. Processed.

————. 1983. "Trade-Related Investment Issues." In Cline, ed.

————. 1985. "Government Control of Foreign Business Investment." In Whalley and Hill, eds.

Schmitz, Andrew, and Colin Carter. 1987. "Sectoral Issues in a US-Canadian Trade Agreement." In Stern, Trezise, and Whalley, forthcoming.

Schott, Jeffrey J. 1983. "Protectionist Threat to Trade and Investment in Services." *World Economy,* vol. 6, no. 2 (June), pp. 195–214.

Sharp, Mitchell. 1972. "Canada-U.S. Relations: Options for the Future." *International Perspectives,* Special Issue (Autumn).

Shearer, R.A., J.H. Young, and G.R. Munro. 1971. *Trade Liberalization and a Regional Economy: Studies of the Impact of Free Trade on British Columbia.* Toronto: University of Toronto Press for the Private Planning Association of Canada.

Spence, A.M. 1977. "Efficiency, Scale and Trade in Canadian and United States Manufacturing Industries." In *Studies in Canadian Industrial Organization.* Edited by Richard E. Caves et al. Ottawa: Study for the Royal Commission on Corporate Concentration.

Stern, Robert M., Phillip H. Trezise, and John Whalley. 1987. *Perspectives on US-Canada Free Trade.* Washington: Brookings, Dialogues on Public Policy.

Trezise, Philip H. 1985. "Relevance of the AutoPact to Other Sectoral Arrangements." *Canada-US Law Journal,* vol. 10, pp. 63–74.

US Congress. House. Committee on Ways and Means, Subcommittee on Trade. 1984. *Overview of Current Provisions of US Trade Law.* 98th Cong., 2d Sess. Washington.

US Department of Commerce, International Trade Administration. 1986a. *Certain Fresh Atlantic Groundfish from Canada: Final Countervailing Duty Determination.* Fed. Reg., vol. 51, no. 56 (24 March), pp. 10041–69. Washington.

————. 1986b . *Preliminary Affirmative Countervailing Duty Determination: Certain Softwood Lumber Products from Canada.* C–122–602, October. Washington.

US International Trade Commission. 1976. *Report on the US-Canadian Automotive*

Agreement: Its History, Terms, and Impact. Printed in US Congress, Senate Committee on Finance. *Canadian Automobile Agreement.* 94th Cong., 1st Sess. Washington.

———. 1985. *Conditions Relating to the Importation of Softwood Lumber into the United States.* Publication 1965, October. Washington.

US Trade Representative. 1981. *North American Trade Agreements.* Study Mandated in Section 1104 of the Trade Agreements Act of 1979. Washington, 4 August. Processed.

———. 1985. *Report to the President on Bilateral Trade with Canada.* Reprinted in Department of External Affairs, 1985.

Viner, Jacob. 1937. *Studies in the Theory of International Trade.* New York, NY: Harper.

———. 1950. *The Customs Union Issue.* New York, NY: Carnegie Endowment for International Peace.

Waite Peter. 1971. *Canada 1874–1896: Arduous Destiny.* Toronto: McClelland and Stewart.

Whalley, John. 1984. " 'Trade, Industrial Policy, and Canadian Manufacturing' by Richard G. Harris (with the assistance of David Cox): A Review Article." *Canadian Journal of Economics,* vol. 17, no. 2 (May), pp. 386–98.

Whalley, John, and Roderick Hill. 1985. *Canada–United States Free Trade.* Toronto: University of Toronto Press, published in cooperation with the Royal Commission on the Economic Union and Development Prospects for Canada.

White, Robert. 1986. "Auto Pact Protects, Free Trade Does Not." *Financial Post* (Toronto), 26 July, p. 8.

Wigle, Randall. 1986. "General Equilibrium Evaluation of Canada-US Liberalization in a Global Context." Paper presented at the meetings of the Canadian Economics Association, Winnipeg, 29 May. Processed.

Wonnacott, Paul. 1965. "Canadian Automotive Protection: Content Provisions, The Bladen Plan, and Export Incentives." *Canadian Journal of Economics and Political Science,* vol. 31, no. 1 (February), pp. 412–27.

———. 1986. "Free Trade Between the United States and Canada: The US Stake." Paper prepared for the Canada–United States Relations Committee, US Chamber of Commerce, March. Processed.

Wonnacott, Ronald J., and Paul Wonnacott. 1967. *Free Trade Between the United States and Canada: The Potential Economic Effects.* Cambridge, Mass.: Harvard University Press.

———. 1981. "Is Unilateral Tariff Reduction Preferable to a Customs Union? The Curious Case of the Missing Foreign Tariffs." *American Economic Review,* vol. 71, no. 4 (September), pp. 704–14.

———. 1982. "Free Trade between the United States and Canada: Fifteen Years Later." *Canadian Public Policy,* Supplement (October).

Young, John H. 1957. *Canadian Commercial Policy.* Ottawa: Royal Commission on Canada's Economic Prospects.

APPENDIX

A FEER for the Canadian Dollar

John Williamson

Appendix   A FEER for the Canadian Dollar
John Williamson

It is argued in chapter 1 that the efficiency gains offered by free trade require a monetary environment where the competitive position of different producers reflects their comparative advantage. This does not mean that exchange rates have to be frozen. However, it does mean that producers need reasonable assurance of the real (inflation-adjusted) exchange rate that will prevail in the long run and a measure of confidence that deviations from this rate will not be substantial. The purpose of this appendix is to estimate what exchange rate would best satisfy these criteria.

It would, of course, be misleading to pretend that the long-run equilibrium real exchange rate will be independent of circumstances. The notion that there is some unique exchange rate that satisfies "purchasing power parity" dies hard, but it finds no theoretical support outside of blatantly unrealistic models that assume the "Law of One Price" (perfect arbitrage) to hold in all markets rather than just those for a few primary commodities. In general, (prolonged) real shocks call for changes in the real exchange rate. For example, a permanent adverse change in the terms of trade normally requires a real depreciation in order to create the incentives to redirect output to the foreign market and to redirect purchases toward domestic producers so as to reverse the deterioration in the balance of trade. Again, an increased savings rate not matched by an increase in domestic investment requires a real depreciation in order to generate the increased trade balance needed to transfer the savings abroad rather than allow them to be wasted in a fall in capacity utilization. But while long-run equilibrium real exchange rates, or "fundamental equilibrium exchange rates" (FEERs), may not be perfectly constant through time, they certainly do not jump around like market exchange rates.

Estimating a FEER requires judgmental inputs, as may be appreciated by reflecting on its definition as that rate "which is expected to

155

FIGURE A.1   **Canada, nominal effective exchange rate**

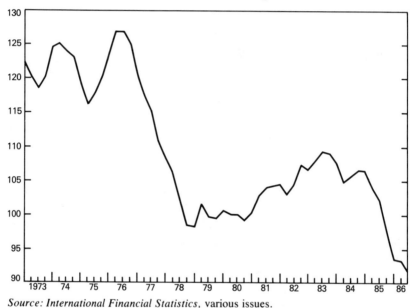

Source: International Financial Statistics, various issues.

generate a current account surplus or deficit equal to the underlying capital flow over the cycle, given that the country is pursuing 'internal balance' as best it can and not restricting trade for balance of payments reasons" (Williamson 1985a, p. 14). The incorporation of normative judgments inevitably makes such an exercise controversial. It is nevertheless an essential exercise if governments are going to accept a responsibility for ensuring that competitive positions are not wildly distorted by macroeconomic events, which may well be a necessary condition for free trade to be politically acceptable.

A natural first step in estimating a FEER is to examine the past behavior of exchange rates. Figure A.1 therefore shows the behavior of the nominal effective exchange rate for the Canadian dollar since 1973; it can be seen that its value in mid-1986 was the lowest ever recorded, over 25 percent below its pre-1977 value. Figure A.2, which shows the evolution of the real effective rate since 1973, reveals that a part of this depreciation served only to offset more rapid inflation in

FIGURE A.2   **Canada, real effective exchange rate**

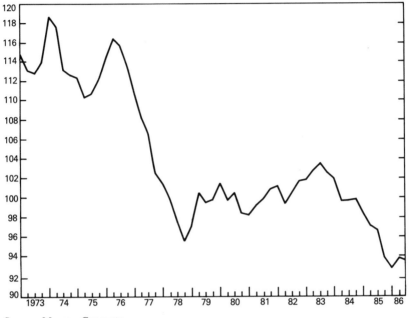

Source: Morgan Guaranty.

Canada than in its main trading partners. Nevertheless, in real terms, as measured by the Morgan index, the Canadian dollar was in October 1986 over 10 percent below its average value for the period 1968–85.

Other measures of the real effective exchange rate are provided by the International Monetary Fund (IMF) cost and price comparisons in manufacturing. Five of these series since 1968 are shown in table A.1, together with the Morgan Guaranty index (which is based on wholesale prices). The behavior of the various indices is surprisingly disparate, but all the measures except that based on relative value-added deflators concur that Canada has in 1986 been extremely competitive by historical standards. And all the measures agree that depreciation has brought a substantial gain in competitiveness, of at least 7 percent, since 1984.

My approach to estimating FEERs involves asking what changes would be needed to achieve (or, when looking back, what changes

TABLE A.1 **Alternative measures of the Canadian real effective exchange rate, 1968–86**
(1980 = 100)

	Morgan Guaranty (WPIs)	IMF unit labor costs	IMF normalized ULCs	IMF value added deflators	IMF WPIs	IMF export unit values
1968	n.a.	111.2	109.5	99.8	111.1	135.3
1969	n.a.	108.0	108.2	98.4	111.5	134.1
1970	104.8	109.5	109.4	100.0	112.9	132.5
1971	106.2	111.2	111.5	101.5	114.8	127.3
1972	108.5	112.4	110.3	103.8	115.6	123.9
1973	111.1	109.1	106.5	105.0	113.4	120.4
1974	117.4	111.5	112.9	112.3	116.4	115.5
1975	112.3	112.5	108.9	105.0	112.0	107.2
1976	116.6	124.1	121.6	112.0	117.3	112.1
1977	108.6	115.1	114.9	104.4	109.4	105.6
1978	100.8	102.4	102.5	96.0	101.3	100.0
1979	100.5	98.3	100.3	96.9	100.5	96.2
1980	100.0	100.0	100.0	100.0	100.0	100.0
1981	99.6	107.3	107.5	108.6	102.3	98.2
1982	100.7	115.9	110.3	113.1	105.5	94.4
1983	102.7	121.0	115.9	118.6	109.5	93.3
1984	100.3	113.1	114.9	118.4	107.8	90.3
1985	96.6	109.4	108.7	115.2	104.6	86.0
1986 Q2	93.7	102.2	99.7	108.7	99.7	77.5
1986 October	93.0	n.a.	n.a.	n.a.	n.a.	n.a.
Av., 1968–85	105.7	110.7	109.7	106.1	109.2	109.6

n.a. Not available.
Source: Morgan Guaranty Bank, *World Financial Markets;* International Monetary Fund, *International Financial Statistics.*

would have been needed to have achieved) a satisfactory payments outcome. When making a forward-looking estimate, this involves examining projections of the current account balance and asking how the exchange rate would need to differ from that assumed in the projection if the current balance were to be shifted to its target value and output were to be at internal balance in the medium term.[1] This requires:

- projections of the current account balance

- a view of the sustainable or optimal current balance, the counterpart to the underlying capital flow

- a view of where the domestic and foreign economies lie relative to "internal balance"

- estimates of the medium-run sensitivity of the current account balance to changes in incomes and prices.

These topics are discussed in turn. The estimates presented draw on published sources and conversations held in late May, 1986 with officials in the Bank of Canada, the Canadian Department of Finance, the Conference Board of Canada, the Ontario Ministry of Treasury and Economics, the International Monetary Fund, and the Federal Reserve Board, as well as academic economists at the C.D. Howe Institute and the Institute for Policy Analysis. Several of the individuals concerned, as well as my colleagues at the Institute for International Economics, were kind enough to comment on a first draft of this paper; I am grateful to them all, but the usual disclaimer about the results being solely my own responsibility is in this instance unusually apt.

The final section of the paper draws the material together to estimate the FEER.

CURRENT ACCOUNT PROJECTIONS

Prior to 1981, Canada was invariably a deficit country on current account. Deficits averaged US\$6.3 billion (in 1983 dollars) in the 1974–79 cycle, as capital flowed in to sustain massive investment in capital-

---

1. Note that this method differs from that adopted in Williamson (1985a), which was backward-looking rather than forward-looking. Specifically, on that occasion I sought to estimate those real exchange rates that would have achieved a set of consistent and apparently reasonable targets for the current account balances of the major countries in 1976–77, and then updated by a PPP extrapolation modified by allowances for major real changes in the world economy (such as oil price changes and the coming on stream of North Sea oil).

T A B L E A.2   **Current account balance, actual and projected**
(billion Canadian dollars)

	1981	1982	1983	1984	1985	1986	1987	1988	1989	1990
Canadian concept	−6.1	2.9	2.9	3.4	−0.6	−5.4	−3.5	−0.5	2.8	5.8
Including retained earnings	−10.2	−1.2	−2.7	−1.7	−5.6	n.a.	n.a.	n.a.	n.a.	n.a.

n.a. Not available.
Source: Bank of Canada for historical figures in row 1; Dungan, MacGregor and Plourde (1986, table 3) for projections in row 1; estimates made by the Treasury Office in the US Embassy, Ottawa, for the modifications in row 2.

intensive energy and minerals projects. As shown in table A.2, these large deficits were transformed into significant surpluses (measured by the Canadian convention, which excludes retained earnings) with the onset of Canada's deepest postwar recession in 1982. Surpluses were sustained through 1984, as recovery was outpaced by that in the United States and as exports were stimulated by the competitive exchange rate against the US dollar (though not against other currencies). A small current account deficit returned in 1985 and became sizable in 1986: the estimate given in table A.2 looks modest in the light of subsequent data. The two dominant causes are a cyclical catchup in growth, which at 4.5 percent exceeded that in the United States by 2.3 percent in 1985; and a further deterioration in the terms of trade, which brought the total decline since 1980 to the first quarter of 1986 to some 15 percent.

The first row of table A.2 also shows the May 1986 projections (using the Canadian concept) for the current account made by the Policy and Economic Analysis Program of the Institute for Policy Analysis (IPA), to 1990. The deficits anticipated for 1986 and 1987 were in the same range as those expected in May by most of the other forecasters with whom the author spoke, although one organization at that time was predicting a return to surplus already in 1987. Subsequent information has suggested that the 1986 deficit will be substantially larger than expected in May; the trade surplus in the first three quarters fell by over 50 percent, which is more than $8 billion at an annual rate, suggesting that the total deficit could easily exceed $8 billion.[2]

A second and striking feature of the IPA projections is the strong trend toward a strengthening current account that they show out to 1990, and indeed to 1992 (followed by a very gradual decline to the end of the forecast period in 1995). A similar strengthening trend, almost invariably of at least $1 billion per year and typically of around $2 billion per year, was postulated by almost all the other forecasters. This appears to reflect both an expectation of a further strengthening in the resource products where Canada is a net exporter and a reduction in its traditional deficit in manufactures. See table A.3 for a summary of the structure of Canadian trade. The strengthening trend is presumably caused partly by the empirical consensus that the income elasticity of foreign demand for Canadian exports exceeds the Canadian income elasticity of demand for imports (see below). In large part, however, it is a lagged response to the recent depreciation. This strong trend occurs even though the IPA has substantially adjusted down the boost to net exports resulting from depreciation below the level suggested by the formal equation in the FOCUS models (Dungan, MacGregor, and Plourde 1986, p. 35).

The IPA's projection of a substantial medium-run current account surplus rests on three principal assumptions:

- a constant bilateral nominal exchange rate of C$1 = US71.5¢, with inflation virtually identical in Canada (average 3.1 percent) as in the United States (average 3.2 percent) in 1986–90, and an effective exchange rate depreciating in both nominal and real terms at about 1.5 percent per year as the DM and yen appreciate against the US and Canadian dollars

- a further 1 percent deterioration in the terms of trade in 1987, followed by essentially constant terms of trade

- very similar real rates of growth in Canada and the United States in the period 1986–90, both averaging about 3 percent per year.

---

2. US trade data show a widening of the bilateral deficit with Canada during 1986, but the Canadian data show the opposite. Reconciliation of the two sets of figures has in the past shown the Canadian data to be the more reliable.

T A B L E A.3 **Structure of Canadian trade, 1985**

Goods	Export composition (percentage)	Balance of trade (billion Canadian dollars)
Food	9	4.2
Energy	14	10.4
Other products with a natural resource base		16.6
Forest products	13	n.a.
Metals and minerals	12	n.a.
Chemicals and fertilizers	4	n.a.
Autos	28	1.5
Other manufactured products	18	− 17.3
Miscellaneous	2	2.0
Subtotal	100	17.5
Services		
Investment income	n.a.	− 14.6
Travel	n.a.	− 2.1
Freight and shipping	n.a.	0.5
Other services and transfers	n.a.	− 1.8
Subtotal	—	− 18.1
Current account balance	—	− 0.6

n.a. Not available.
Note: Figures may not sum to totals owing to rounding.
Source: "Balance of Payments Developments in 1985," *Bank of Canada Review* (June 1986), tables II and V, updated with subsequent data revisions.

Most other forecasters were assuming either a constant dollar exchange rate or some modest appreciation of the Canadian dollar; either constant terms of trade or a modest recovery of up to 1 percent per year; and either similar growth to that in the United States or slightly faster Canadian growth. Thus the IPA's exchange rate and growth assumptions tend to enlarge the current account projection as compared to a number of other forecasters, but its more critical terms of trade assumption is at the pessimistic end of the spectrum. Most other forecasters believed that the terms of trade deterioration had already run its course, and that, while no major recovery could be projected, some modest improvement was more likely than not.

Although the IPA projections start off from a somewhat modest estimate of the deficit, overall they seem to afford a reasonable basis on which to construct an estimate of a FEER. They assume an essentially constant real exchange rate against the US dollar and a modest effective real depreciation. And they are based on assumptions that are seemingly reasonable and fairly close to the prevailing consensus. The most likely major deviation from the assumptions (other than that pertaining to the exchange rate) would involve a faster recovery in the terms of trade as a result of a rise in the prices of some of the primary products of which Canada is a net exporter. Such an event would be likely both to raise growth and to improve the balance of payments relative to current projections.

CURRENT ACCOUNT TARGET

Canada has traditionally been a net capital importer on a significant scale, to the point where debt service now costs it $15 billion per year (table A.3). Its rapid development at the beginning of the twentieth century drew very heavily on foreign savings. More recently, it borrowed extensively to finance capital-intensive resource projects (in energy and minerals) during the late 1970s. Those projects have now come on stream, and the low current and expected prices for both energy and minerals have prevented a follow-up wave of investment. The expectation is that any expansion of investment in the next few years will be directed toward manufacturing, which is much less capital intensive.

As far as savings are concerned, personal savings have recently been higher than in the United States: the personal savings rate exceeded 15 percent in 1982 and was almost 11 percent in 1985 (as against 7 percent and 5 percent, respectively, in the United States). Offsetting this fairly high savings rate has been a substantial federal fiscal deficit in recent years, about 6 percent of GNP in 1985. The 1986 budget announced a medium-run program aimed at reducing the federal fiscal deficit to some 2.5 percent of GNP by 1990. This is a fiscal adjustment of the same magnitude as that achieved in Europe and

Japan in the first half of the 1980s so that, although it would involve a substantial effort, there is no reason to dismiss it as infeasible.

If private savings remain high while public dissaving is reduced and investment remains subdued, there will be a case for Canada to emerge as a capital exporter with a regular current account surplus in order to avoid the danger that the economy will be pushed into permanent recession. Many Canadians with whom the author spoke do seem to believe that Canada has reached the stage at which it is desirable and natural for Canada to export rather than import capital, at least on a modest scale.

There are, however, several counterarguments:

International compatibility. Other countries are going to have to shave their current account targets in order to accommodate the needed improvement in the US current account, and Canada should accept its share of the "burden."

Errors in balance of payments statistics. The world currently has a recorded current account deficit of some US$80 billion, because recorded payments for services exceed receipts. If Canada has a share of those missing receipts equal to its share in global exports of services, its current account position is being underrecorded by some $2.7 billion per year.

Uncertain assumptions. It was argued above that the most likely significant deviation from the assumptions used to project the current account would involve improved terms of trade and hence a stronger current account.

Demography. With population growth of almost 1 percent per year and labor-force growth still in excess of 1 percent per year, Canada is one of the industrial countries where demographic factors suggest investment should be high relative to savings.

Neo-Ricardian theorem. One expects that a part of any increase in public saving will be offset by a reduction in private saving.

These considerations make it difficult to regard Canada as a natural capital exporter at this stage, although neither should it be expected to revert to the position of a major capital importer. A balanced current account would seem a fairly natural objective. Unfortunately this phrase is ambiguous in the Canadian context, since Canada measures its current account without deducting an estimate for retained earnings of direct investment. The sum involved is quite substantial, around $5 billion per year, as shown in the second row of table A.2. Thus, a reasonable range of estimates of the target current account balance on the measured Canadian concept would be from a surplus of $5 billion per year to a deficit of $3 billion (reflecting unrecorded receipts): the central estimate that will be used in the calculations is the mid-point, a surplus of $1 billion per year.

INTERNAL BALANCE

Canadian estimates of the NAIRU[3] are typically around 6 percent, although some estimates are as high as 8 percent. Canadian unemployment is substantially higher than this at the moment, around 9.5 percent. This is a much larger gap than exists in Canada's dominant trading partner, the United States, where unemployment of about 7 percent is perhaps 1 percent above the NAIRU. But the gap is lower than in some of Canada's other trading partners, notably in Europe.

The IPA model projects declining unemployment in Canada, but only to 9.3 percent in 1990 and 7.3 percent in 1995. These figures tend to suggest a need for more expansionary policies. However, this conclusion is controversial in Canada, on account of the geographical distribution of unemployment. Unemployment in Ontario (about 40 percent of the Canadian economy) is only some 6 percent to 7 percent, close to the estimated NAIRU. It could be argued that the Ontario NAIRU is probably lower than that for the Canadian economy as a whole, but some observers argue that there are already signs of inflationary strains in Ontario (such as wage increases accelerating to 5 percent per year or more). Industrial Quebec also had a strong recovery. In contrast, the areas dependent on resource extraction, like Alberta (oil), British Columbia, and the maritime provinces, have extremely high unemployment rates (and near-zero wage inflation). While unemployment has traditionally been high in the maritime provinces, this is not true of the west.

A recovery of the prices of resource products would simultaneously ease the geographical disparities in unemployment and improve the

---

3. The "nonaccelerating inflation rate of unemployment," often referred to as the "natural rate of unemployment."

balance of payments. In the absence of such a recovery, views differ on whether demand management policy should seek to do much to hasten the decline in unemployment. There is reportedly a problem of excessive real wages in many of the areas that have now lost their prosperity, and adjustment will require that real wage aspirations be pruned back, and that production-location decisions respond to the changed structure of real wages. If Western Canada had its own currency, this process might be hastened by a depreciation of its dollar in relation to that of Eastern Canada. But it is doubtful in the extreme whether it would be wise to seek a substitute mechanism through encouraging a resumption of inflation in Ontario and Quebec: we have now learned that stopping inflation is also extremely expensive in terms of unemployment. It has to be recognized that the Canadian NAIRU cannot be considered a constant but is sensitive to the structure of world demand, and that recent changes have had the effect of raising the NAIRU, at least for some time.

In view of this analysis, it would seem inappropriate to give much weight to a need to reflate in Canada relative to its principal trading partners. A reasonable aim might be to seek reflation adequate to reduce unemployment to a high estimate of the NAIRU, say 8 percent. Applying an Okun's coefficient of 2 would point to a need for additional output of 2.6 percent by 1990. But unemployment is also unacceptably high in some of Canada's trading partners, notably in Europe: if one assumes that a cyclical fall in European unemployment should raise output there by an additional 6 percent by 1990, the Canadian cyclical allowance is shaved to about 1.5 percent of GNP.

Larger reductions in unemployment will either occur automatically, if resource prices rise, and be (more than) self-financing in a payments sense, or else they will inevitably be lengthy, and already allowed for in the projected decline of unemployment to 7.3 percent in 1995.

INCOME AND PRICE ELASTICITIES

Estimates of the income elasticities of demand for Canadian exports and imports seem to vary from about unity to 1.7, with most estimates nearer the bottom end of the range and with the export elasticity typically somewhat larger than the import elasticity (contributing to the forecasts of an improving current account balance over time). The only exceptions are where estimates have been made for bilateral Canadian trade with individual countries: estimates of income elasticities with some of Canada's smaller trading partners, like Japan and the United Kingdom, span a substantially wider range.

Views on price elasticities are more difficult to compare. Some estimates are disaggregated by commodity, others by trading partner. Different assumptions are made about price responses to real exchange rate changes. But even allowing for these factors, some real differences of view seem to exist: for example, some believe that auto exports are more price-sensitive than other manufactures, others that they are less (at least outside of a certain range, where the terms of the US-Canadian Auto Pact come into play in limiting responses to relative prices). Estimates of the import-price elasticity seem to vary from about -0.7 to -1.5. Estimates of the price elasticity of demand for manufactured exports vary from about -0.5 to -1.5, with estimates for some resource products lower still. (In some cases, however, it seems to be assumed that Canadian export prices are effectively determined by world prices, so that the estimated elasticity must really be a supply elasticity.)

In order to estimate the impact of a real depreciation on the balance of payments one needs one more figure, namely an assumption for the value of the "pass-through coefficient" that measures the proportion of a devaluation that is passed through into a reduction in foreign prices. This coefficient tends to be close to 1 for a continental economy like the United States and is zero in the textbook case of the small open economy. Canada clearly falls between these extremes. A value of 0.5 is unlikely to be very far from the mark.

The impact of a 10 percent depreciation on the 1990 trade balance measured in Canadian dollars then comprises the following four elements:

$$\begin{matrix} \textit{Value of} \\ \textit{increased export} \\ \textit{volume} \end{matrix} = \begin{matrix} \textit{Elasticity of} \\ \textit{demand for} \\ \textit{exports} \end{matrix} \times \begin{matrix} \textit{Change in} \\ \textit{FX price} \\ \textit{of exports} \end{matrix} \times \begin{matrix} \textit{Initial} \\ \textit{value of} \\ \textit{exports} \end{matrix}$$

$$= \begin{Bmatrix} 1.5 \\ 0.5 \end{Bmatrix} \times 0.05 \times 185 = \begin{Bmatrix} 13.9 \\ 4.6 \end{Bmatrix}.$$

$$\begin{array}{c} \textit{Increased export} \\ \textit{revenue from} \\ \textit{higher prices} \end{array} = \begin{array}{c} \textit{Proportionate change} \\ \textit{in C\$ export} \\ \textit{price} \end{array} \times \begin{array}{c} \textit{Initial} \\ \textit{value of} \\ \textit{exports} \end{array}$$

$$= 0.05 \times 185 = 9.3.$$

$$\begin{array}{c} \textit{Value of} \\ \textit{decline in} \\ \textit{import volume} \end{array} = \begin{array}{c} \textit{Elasticity of} \\ \textit{demand for} \\ \textit{imports} \end{array} \times \begin{array}{c} \textit{Proportionate} \\ \textit{change in} \\ \textit{C\$ import price} \end{array} \times \begin{array}{c} \textit{Initial value} \\ \textit{of imports} \end{array}$$

$$= \left\{ \begin{array}{c} 1.5 \\ 0.7 \end{array} \right\} \times 0.1 \times 150 = \left\{ \begin{array}{c} 22.5 \\ 10.5 \end{array} \right\}.$$

$$\begin{array}{c} \textit{Increased import} \\ \textit{cost from higher} \\ \textit{prices} \end{array} = \begin{array}{c} \textit{Proportionate change} \\ \textit{in C\$ import price} \end{array} \times \begin{array}{c} \textit{Initial value} \\ \textit{of imports} \end{array}$$

$$= 0.1 \times 150 = 15.$$

Summing the first three terms and subtracting the last gives the estimated medium-run effect of a 10 percent real depreciation with 1990 trade values as between $30.7 billion (with high elasticities) and $9.4 billion (with low elasticities). (The comparable range for the impact on the trade balance as measured in foreign exchange is between US$27.1 billion and US$5.8 billion.)

One can also extract estimates of the impact of a sustained depreciation on the Canadian current account from some large models. The IMF multilateral exchange rate model (MERM) was specifically constructed for such exercises. Taking the estimate presented on the basis of 1977 data in Artus and McGuirk (1981, table 8) and multiplying up by the expected increase in the value of trade from 1977 to 1990 (a factor of 3.05), the estimated impact of a 10 percent nominal devaluation would be US$7.8 billion to US$10.8 billion. My own preference would be for the higher of those figures, which makes normal price elasticity assumptions and assumes a relatively low price feedback. The MERM estimate seems consistent with the range of figures derived from the preceding back-of-the-envelope calculation (since that related to a *real* depreciation).

However, this figure is at the high end of the range of estimates presented at a conference where the properties of alternative Canadian macroeconometric models were compared. The set of estimates of the effect after 5 years of a sustained nominal devaluation of 10 percent resulting from a portfolio shock rather than a relaxation of monetary policy were as follows:

Model	Effect in 1982 (billion Canadian dollars)	Implied effect in 1990 (billion Canadian dollars)
QFS (Department of Finance)	2.3	5.1
RDXF (Bank of Canada)	4.0	8.9
DRI	5.8	12.9
TIME	2.9	6.5
CANDIDE 2.0	4.1	9.2
SAM	1.8	4.0
MACE	− 6.3	− 14.0

Source: O'Reilly, Paulin, and Smith (1983), shock 9B, p. 55.

Even ignoring the perverse (and outlying) estimate of the MACE model, these figures show a great deal of variation with a relatively modest mean. The second lowest figure from those models, C$5.1 billion, will be taken as a lower bound; C$12 billion will be taken as a central estimate; and C$30 billion will be taken as the upper bound.

ESTIMATING THE FEER

The estimates presented above suggest that with the present pattern of exchange rates, and the present outlook for fiscal-monetary policies, Canada can expect a current account surplus as conventionally measured in Canada of the order of C$6 billion by 1990.

It was suggested in the discussion on internal balance that prospective Canadian conjunctural policy is on the tight side, and ideally ought to allow for an additional output expansion of perhaps 2.6 percent by 1990, of which 1.5 percent would be a net effect after allowing for a similar factor in Europe. Using a conventional estimate of unity for the income elasticity of demand, additional imports of some C$2.2

billion would have to be expected if output were indeed to grow enough to reduce unemployment to 8 percent. Thus the current account surplus would be reduced to about C$4 billion.

This figure has to be compared to the desirable current account target. The previous discussion of that subject concluded that (in terms of the conventional measure) a reasonable central estimate of a target for the Canadian current account would be a surplus of C$1 billion per year, with a range from a deficit of C$3 billion to a C$5 billion surplus.

The range of estimates of the deviation in the value of the Canadian dollar from its FEER is shown in table A.4. Thus, depending on whether one is an elasticity optimist or pessimist and on one's view of the current account adjustment needed, one might regard either a 14 percent appreciation or a 2 percent depreciation from the exchange rate embodied in the IPA forecast as appropriate. The central estimate is for an appreciation of 3 percent.

The IPA exchange rate assumptions involve a bilateral exchange rate against the US dollar that is constant at C$1 = US 71.5¢ combined with a continuing depreciation of the US dollar against the yen and the European currencies. Thus, the effective rate of the Canadian dollar is projected to depreciate from 130 in 1985 to 140 in 1986 and 150 in 1990. However, since trade flows respond to exchange rate changes with a lag, the relevant base from which to calculate the desirable appreciation is not the 1990 index of 150 but (perhaps) the 1988 index of 144. On this reckoning, the index corresponding to fundamental equilibrium would be 140 on the IPA index and 70 on the Bank of Canada index against the Group of Ten currencies, suggesting that the real effective exchange rate was about right in the second quarter of 1986.

According to my earlier calculations (Williamson 1985a, p. 79), the US dollar still needed to fall another 8 percent in effective terms in order to achieve fundamental equilibrium (as of October 1986). (This would take it to a value of 91 on Morgan Guaranty's real effective exchange rate index.) The implication of the preceding calculation is that it would be inappropriate for the Canadian dollar to fall in effective terms if the US dollar declines. Since the US dollar has a weighting of about 70 percent in the Canadian effective rate, the 8 percent depreciation of the US dollar that still seems to be called for would require an appreciation of the bilateral rate of the Canadian dollar in terms of the US dollar of rather under 3.5 percent from the mid-1985 figure of 71.5¢ to hold the Canadian effective rate constant. Thus, my estimate of the bilateral equilibrium rate against the US dollar is C$1 = 74¢.

This result may surprise others, as it has surprised me. When I started this exercise I expected to end favoring a substantially stronger rate, in the range of 75¢ to 80¢; indeed, a previous preliminary foray of mine (Williamson 1985b, p. 262) had implied a figure of around 85¢ as appropriate. There has, however, been a major and highly relevant exogenous change in the intervening period, namely the 9 percent deterioration in the Canadian terms of trade due to the weakening in energy and other primary product prices. In the absence of a central expectation that this worsening will be reversed during the next decade, it is necessary that it be reflected in a more competitive exchange rate. With the central elasticity assumption, a $17 billion "permanent" loss from terms of trade deterioration would need a 14 percent depreciation to offset it.

Table A.4 illustrates the fact that the outcome of an exercise like this is dependent on a large number of assumptions about which there is ample scope for disagreement. This is one reason why it would be unwise to try to force the market rate to remain close to the estimated equilibrium rate. (Other reasons include the desirability of leaving some scope for monetary policy to be directed toward domestic ends and the need to be sure that one does not get into a position of defending a disequilibrium rate against speculative pressures.) For such reasons, I have suggested that target zones of ± 10 percent be defined around FEERs, and that policy attempt to ensure that rates

TABLE A.4   **Range of estimates of desirable appreciation of Canadian dollar**

Elasticities	Size of current account adjustment needed		
	−7	−3	+1
Low	+14	+6	−2
Central	+6	+3	−1
High	+2	+1	0

do not normally go outside such zones. On this criterion, the Canadian authorities' decision of February 1986 to prevent the rate from falling below 69¢ appears opportune. The authorities used the right instrument at the right time for the right purpose and did indeed reverse an undue weakening of the Canadian dollar, at a tolerable cost. Their actions might have been even more effective, or conceivably even redundant, had a formal target-zone mechanism been in place, but in any event the defense of the Canadian dollar provides a good instance of the sort of policy adjustments that a target-zone system would call for.

The failure of the initial depreciation of the US dollar to bring as rapid a turnaround in the US balance of payments as optimists had hoped for has sparked a search for explanations. Fingers have been pointed at Canada, as well as at some of the newly industrializing countries (NICs), because of the failure of their currencies to appreciate in parallel with the yen and the European currencies. Whatever truth there may be in such accusations against the NICs, it is important to the prospects of harmonious US-Canadian trade negotiations that it be understood that there was a good reason why the Canadian dollar did not strengthen. While the Canadian dollar appears to have been marginally weaker against the US dollar in 1986 than would be ideal from the standpoint of long-run trade considerations, the difference was well within the range of error inherent in these types of calculations, as well as within a reasonable target zone. In preventing a further decline in February 1986, Canada helped create the monetary conditions that would permit free trade between the United States and Canada. What remains is to formalize an agreement that ensures that both countries continue to act in this spirit.

References

Artus, Jacques R., and Anne Kenny McGuirk. 1981. "A Revised Version of the Multilateral Exchange Rate Model." IMF *Staff Papers,* vol. 28, no. 2 (June).

Dungan, Peter, Mary MacGregor, and Andre Plourde. 1986. *National Projections Through 1995.* Policy Study No. 86–5 (University of Toronto Institute for Policy Analysis). Processed.

O'Reilly, Brian, Graydon Paulin, and Philip Smith. 1983. "Responses of Various Econometric Models to Selected Policy Shocks." Bank of Canada *Technical Report* 38. Processed.

Williamson, John. 1985a. *The Exchange Rate System,* 2d ed. POLICY ANALYSES IN INTERNATIONAL ECONOMICS 5 (Washington: Institute for International Economics), rev. June.

————. (1985b), "Exchange Rate Misalignments, Trade and Canadian Policy." In *Domestic Policies in the International Economic Environment.* Edited by John Whalley. (Toronto: University of Toronto Press in cooperation with the Royal Commission on the Economic Union and Development Prospects for Canada.)

Other Publications from the Institute

POLICY ANALYSES IN INTERNATIONAL ECONOMICS SERIES

Economic Sanctions Reconsidered: History and Current Policy
Gary Clyde Hufbauer and Jeffrey J. Schott, assisted by Kimberly Ann Elliott/
1985

Trade Protection in the United States: 31 Case Studies
Gary Clyde Hufbauer, Diane T. Berliner, and Kimberly Ann Elliott/1986

Toward Renewed Economic Growth in Latin America
Bela Balassa, Gerardo M. Bueno, Pedro-Pablo Kuczynski, and Mario Henrique Simonsen/1986

American Trade Politics: System Under Stress
I.M. Destler/1986

SPECIAL REPORTS

1   **Promoting World Recovery: A Statement on Global Economic Strategy** *by Twenty-six Economists from Fourteen Countries*/December 1982

2   **Prospects for Adjustment in Argentina, Brazil, and Mexico: Responding to the Debt Crisis**
John Williamson, editor/June 1983

3   **Inflation and Indexation: Argentina, Brazil, and Israel**
John Williamson, editor/March 1985

4   **Global Economic Imbalances**
C. Fred Bergsten, editor/March 1986

5   **African Debt and Financing**
Carol Lancaster and John Williamson, editors/May 1986

FORTHCOMING

Capital Flight: The Problem and Policy Responses
Donald R. Lessard and John Williamson

Capital Flight and Third World Debt
Donald R. Lessard and John Williamson, editors

Auction Quotas and US Trade Policy
C. Fred Bergsten and Jeffrey J. Schott

The Future of World Trade in Textiles and Apparel
William R. Cline

Agriculture and the GATT: Issues in a New Trade Round
Dale E. Hathaway

The United States as a Debtor Country
C. Fred Bergsten and Shafiqul Islam

Domestic Adjustment and International Trade
Gary Clyde Hufbauer and Howard F. Rosen, editors

Target Zones and Policy Coordination
Marcus Miller and John Williamson